WHITE STAR LINERS AT WAR

WHITE STAR LINERS AT WAR

A HISTORY THROUGH ILLUSTRATIONS

PATRICK MYLON

The
History
Press

Frontispiece: A well-known aerial view of *Olympic*, possibly 1918, with US or Canadian troops and two 6-inch guns on her stern.

Front cover: Oceanic aground on 8 September 1914 near the Shetland Islands. (Original painting by Neil Egginton)

Back cover: Olympic carrying US troops to Europe on 12 May 1918. (Original painting by Neil Egginton)

First published 2020

The History Press
97 St George's Place, Cheltenham,
Gloucestershire, GL50 3QB
www.thehistorypress.co.uk

British Library Cataloguing in Publication Data.
A catalogue record for this book is available from the British Library.

ISBN 978 0 7509 8811 7

Typesetting and origination by The History Press
Printed in Turkey by Imak

CONTENTS

FOREWORD BY SIR NEVILLE PURVIS KCB, VICE ADMIRAL

This book is an excellent piece of scholarship detailing the participation of the White Star Line ships in wars.

It is a truism that the Merchant Navy has always been the fourth arm of defence in the United Kingdom. The loss of life and general sacrifice made by merchant ships in war has become a remarkable story of dedication by men and women at sea. There is an extraordinary sense of duty by people, whose purpose was trade, when it has come to the hardships of fighting for the country they support. When merchant ships enter war zones, the lives of all aboard are at peril. The determination shown by all ranks to try to survive the savage sea, in conditions which are often extreme, provides an extraordinary background to the rigours of seagoing. Behind every sinking, every engagement, lie tales of great heroism and endeavour.

I commend this work to all who have an interest in the annals of the sea. The White Star Line recorded at the end of the First World War was a triumph of ceaseless efforts demanded by the grim struggle to emerge victorious and also in economic measures of great importance to the national life.

INTRODUCTION

My interest in the White Star Line began, in 1958, when I saw the film *A Night to Remember* about the loss of White Star's liner *Titanic* on her maiden voyage in 1912. Since that time my interest in the line has grown to such an extent that I have collected many postcards of the various ships. Many of these illustrations have been used in my three previously published books: *The White Star Collection: The History of a Shipping Line in Postcards*, *The Unseen* Olympic and *R.M.S.* Titanic: *The Wider Story*.

There was only one book left to write! To be perfectly honest I have used a few of the pictures, but not many, from my previous books. All of the illustrations, except two, in this book belong to me. The three confrontations occurred in 1899–1902, 1914–18 and 1939–45, so the liner that started the whole thing, as far as I was concerned, doesn't even get a look-in! However, her sister ships, *Olympic* and *Britannic*, do feature enormously.

This publication is not aimed at those of you who know much more than myself about the line, but I do hope that you will achieve some enjoyment from reading it. What I would really like to get across is how much one shipping line contributed to its nation during various confrontations.

Where possible I have tried to acknowledge the myriad number of photographers, publishers and printers throughout. If I have accidentally omitted any then do please let me know and I shall ensure that the error is corrected in any future editions.

THE WHITE STAR LINE

On 6 September 1869 the Oceanic Steam Navigation Company (OSNC) was registered. One of the founders, Thomas H. Ismay (died 1899), had bought from a liquidated, predominantly sailing-ship, company the name 'White Star', its goodwill and the house flag which comprised a red burgee with a white star.

An initial order of four ships later added to by two slightly larger vessels, was placed with the ship-building firm of Harland & Wolff in Belfast. From then on, the majority of OSNC's (White Star Line) ships were constructed at Harland & Wolff up to the end of White Star Line, when it merged with the Cunard Line in 1934. The contract between White Star Line and Harland & Wolff stated that all vessels ordered were to be built with the best materials available, cost was to be nett with an agreed profit margin and Harland & Wolff were not to build ships for the competition without White Star Line's permission.

From then on, the funnel colours of buff with black tops became well known in Liverpool and the USA, and later in Australia, New Zealand, South Africa, Canada and others.

In 1902 the White Star Line was taken over by J. Pierpont Morgan's International Mercantile Marine Co. (IMMC). The terms of the purchase were agreed to by J. Bruce Ismay (Chairman and son of Thomas) and seventy-five shareholders. White Star signed an agreement that, after the takeover, her vessels would continue to be registered in Britain for the next twenty years.

During the history of the White Star Line there were two international 'confrontations'. The first was in 1899, known as the Second Boer War, and the second, much greater of course, was the First World War.

In 1926 the Royal Mail Steam Packet Co. secured the entire share capital of the White Star Line from the International Mercantile Marine Co. (now headed by the son of J. Pierpont Morgan) and on 1 January 1927 White Star Line became, once more, a British company.

Having made four consecutive annual financial losses, White Star Line's board met with the board of the Cunard Line on 30 December 1933. Cunard-White Star Ltd was registered on 10 May 1934.

Although the White Star Line and Cunard had merged in 1934 several ex-White Star vessels went on to be active in the Second World War.

'THE UNKNOWN SHIP'

Traffic (1)

Built in Runcorn in 1873, she served the White Star Line as a Liverpool baggage and stores tender for over twenty years before being sold to the Liverpool Lighterage Co. in 1896. Having had her engine removed she was sunk in May 1941 by German bombing. Raised, she was not scrapped until 1955.

1

THE BOER WARS

The first of the two Boer Wars in the Transvaal Republic commenced in 1880. Britain's attempts at annexation were initially thwarted by the Dutch Boers causing several British defeats. The government of British Prime Minister William Gladstone did not wish to involve itself in an overseas war which would require considerable troop movements. It was thought that the expense would not justify the return. Hence there followed an armistice and later a peace treaty was drawn up with Paul Kruger, the President of the Transvaal, in 1881.

The second Boer War, from 11 October 1899 until 31 May 1902, involved the British Empire and two of the Boer states. The Republic of Transvaal and the Orange Free State had come to resent the influence of Britain in South Africa. Initially the Boer confrontations were successful until Britain, and the Empire, began to rush troops to South Africa in greater and greater numbers. Eventually the increasingly harsh British reinforcements caused the South Africans to negotiate a peace settlement.

Although there was no fighting at sea, a considerable number of British shipping companies became involved in the rush to get troops to South Africa. In addition to the movement of soldiers to the battle grounds it was also necessary to transport horses, mules and equipment and also to bring home the dead and wounded.

Earlier in 1899 the White Star Line had originated a service from Liverpool to Cape Town and on to Australia. This service, of three vessels, was increased to five a year later, thus offering a weekly departure. Where possible White Star Line ships were requisitioned to ship men and supplies to and from South Africa using this service.

The duties involving trooping affected the five-ship schedule of *Suevic*, and her four sisters *Afric*, *Medic*, *Persic* and *Runic*. This, however, earned a considerable amount of extra revenue and it was not until the Boer War was over that the scheduled monthly service came into being.

WHITE STAR LINERS IN THE SECOND BOER WAR

Britannic (1)

Built at Belfast, the *Britannic* was initially to be named *Hellenic* but this was changed prior to her launch. She was given taller funnels in 1895, as shown on this postcard, published in Cape Town.

When she was requisitioned as a troopship, in October 1899, she had made her last transatlantic crossing on 16 August. Her first voyage as a troopship was from Queenstown (now Cobh) in Ireland carrying almost 1,000 troops with horses and supplies to Cape Town. On this voyage she was under the command of Bertram Hayes, later to be knighted and to become the Commodore of the White Star Line. In his book *Hull Down* he refers to these troops in that they came down from Belfast somewhat the 'worse for wear' as a result of the send-off that they had been given by the people of Belfast. Prior to boarding the train to Queenstown a considerable amount of whiskey had been drunk!

Officers were accommodated in first-class cabins and the troops in steerage (Third Class). After the initial troop movement was over, nurses followed and officers' wives as 'indulgence' passengers. In all she made ten round-trip voyages to the Cape as well as two to Australia. On 12 November 1900, still in white livery but with her funnel tops painted black she departed for Australia to attend the festivities to mark the creation of the Commonwealth of that country. The situation at the Cape had, by this time, swung in Britain's favour.

After her return to the UK the *Britannic* was sent back to Belfast, but a survey of the vessel confirmed that further modification would not be worth the money. In August 1903 she was towed from Belfast to Hamburg for breaking.

Britannic: Built 1874. Gross tonnage 5,004. HM Transport No.62. Early days as troopship. Photograph taken at Cape Town. Possibly 1899–1900. (M. Leendertz Photographer)

Britannic: Still HM Transport No.62 but with white hull and buff funnels originally, now black-topped funnels. (Published by Real Photographs)

Teutonic

Both *Teutonic* and her sister *Majestic* (1) contributed to the Boer War as transports. *Teutonic* (HMT No.2) in the winter of 1900 and *Majestic* (1), under Capt. E.J. Smith, in December 1899 from Liverpool to Cape Town with 2,000 troops, and then *Majestic* again in February 1900 from Southampton to Cape Town. They had both received a Naval subsidy during their construction at Harland & Wolff and, as a result *Teutonic* was taken into government service as a troopship at the start of the confrontation. Initially *Teutonic* was one of four vessels supplied by the White Star Line. The authorities commended the White Star Line for the two liners getting important numbers of troops to the Cape with such swiftness.

Teutonic: Built 1874. Gross tonnage 9,984. Used as a Boer War transport during the winter of 1900.

Above: Nomadic: Built 1891. Gross tonnage 5,749. The first White Star ship requisitioned as a Boer War troopship and horse transport, No.34. (Nautical Photo Agency)

Nomadic (1)

One of the first vessels to be taken over for trooping and transportation in October 1899. The vessel was allocated the title HM *Transport No.34* and served in this capacity for nearly two years. Amongst the hundreds of horses shipped to the Cape were those requisitioned from London's horse bus operators.

Gothic

The vessel was used for the repatriation of troops on the South Africa–UK and South Africa–New Zealand sections of her normal service in the summer of 1902.

Left: Gothic: Built 1893. Gross tonnage 7,755. Employed as a Boer War repatriation transport on the Cape to UK and NZ portions of her route.

Canada

Built for the Dominion Line service to Canada from the UK, the vessel served as a Boer War transport from 1899 to 1902.

Cymric

The vessel was originally intended to carry emigrants out to the USA from the UK and cattle back but, because of the unpopularity of such an idea at this time, her construction was changed prior to launch to accommodate Third Class each way. She made two trooping voyages to the Cape early in 1900 as HMT *No. 74* but was released from those duties at the end of April.

Canada: Built 1896. Gross tonnage 8,806. Became Boer War transport No.69 as shown here in 1901. (IMMCo)

Cymric: Built 1898. Gross tonnage 13,096. HM *Transport No.74* made the first of two consecutive Boer War trooping voyages from Liverpool to Cape Town on 1 January 1900, with the second sailing on 1 March. (Pictorial Stationery)

THE BOER WARS 15

Persic

On 7 December 1899 the vessel departed Liverpool for Australia carrying 500 troops to S. Africa. Whilst in Cape Town she developed cracks in her rudder casing which had to be repaired before continuing her voyage with sick and wounded Australian troops departing 1 February 1900. On her return to the UK departing 26 April from Australia she brought further horses and troops for service in S. Africa.

Medic

As the *Medic* was about to leave Australia on the return leg of her voyage in 1899 the Boer War had started on 16 October. She was immediately chartered by the Australian government to carry over 600 troops with horses and mules to Cape Town. A large freezing hold was converted to accommodate troops in temporary bunks. The *Medic*, now HMT *No. A7*, departed Australia in a small convoy of four ships to the Cape.

Persic: Built 1899. Gross tonnage 11,973. Took home Australian sick and wounded in 1900. (Nautical Photo Agency)

Medic: Built 1899. Gross tonnage 11,985. On her return maiden voyage she carried Australian troops and their horses to the Boer War.

Victorian

Both the *Victorian* (illustrated) and her sister *Armenian* were launched in 1895 as *Victorian* and *Indian* respectively for the cargo and cattle service of the Leyland Line from Liverpool to Boston. The single-screw vessels worked as Boer War transports throughout the period 1899–1902 transporting mostly horses, after which they resumed their normal service.

Victorian: Built 1895. Gross tonnage 8,825. Leyland Line (Managed by White Star, 1903). Boer War transport mainly used to carry horses to S. Africa. Used extensively until November 1902. Renamed *Russian* in August 1914. (John Clarkson photograph)

Belgic (2)

This vessel was built for the Occidental & Oriental Pacific service. After fourteen years she was sold to the Atlantic Transport Line (IMMC) and renamed *Mohawk* and, as such, she was taken over by the British Government for Boer War service. Upon her release in 1902, the company having decided not to refit her, she was scrapped in Liverpool in 1903. (Not illustrated)

Delphic (1)

The *Delphic* (1) transported 1,200 troops on 31 March 1900 from the UK to Cape Town during her outbound journey to New Zealand. She then made her second trip to the Cape, from Queenstown, on 4 April 1901, once again whilst on the way to New Zealand. (Not illustrated)

Afric

Between 1900 and 1902 the *Afric* transported troops with their horses, from the UK to the Cape, whilst she was on the way to Australia.

Suevic

The *Suevic* was launched at Harland & Wolff on 8 December 1900 and completed on 9 March 1901. She was straight away taken over by the British Government for trooping. Taking over 200 men and a large cargo to the Cape, she continued to Australia repatriating their troops. On her return to the UK she carried more troops from Australia to the Cape. (Not illustrated)

Ionic (1)

She worked the joint Shaw Savill & Albion – White Star service to New Zealand from 1884, crewed by White Star and managed by Shaw Savill. The *Ionic* (1), whilst making her last voyage to New Zealand, carried troops, cavalry and stores to Cape Town for the Boer War in December 1899. She was scrapped in Morecambe in April 1908. (Not illustrated)

Afric: Built 1899. Gross tonnage 11,948. Carried troops to the Cape on the first leg of her journey (Liverpool – Cape Town).

2

THE FIRST WORLD WAR 1914–18

In June of 1914 the UK's merchant marine gross tonnage totalled 18,892,000, whereas that of Germany totalled 5,135,000.

On 28 June 1914 the Austrian Archduke Franz Ferdinand and his wife were assassinated by bullets fired by a Serbian rebel. A month later Austria declared war on Serbia as reprisal. There then followed nearly four and a half years of fighting that involved a majority of the world's nations including, importantly for the White Star Line, Britain and, to a lesser extent, Belgium. One of the last of the countries to enter the conflict was Great Britain, which declared war against Germany and Austria on 4 August 1914 as a result of Germany attacking France. At that time the White Star Line owned, or managed, thirty-five ships, all of which were to serve, at one time or another, their country.

Despite the fact that enormous land fighting took place in Europe, it was at sea that the Allies were able to secure transport and supply. With the arrival of the USA to the European theatre of war in April 1917, the vessels required to ship nearly two million men, supply them and also to supply foreign armies and civilians were innumerable. Sea warfare therefore was not just the confrontation of battle fleets but the struggle of the Allied Mercantile Marine against enemy submarines, mines and surface raiders.

After the end of the Boer War in 1902, the UK had not been involved in any major conflict until the outbreak of the First World War in 1914. As far as shipping was concerned this was to change dramatically on a global scale. All over the world large luxury liners were to change their roles into Armed Merchant Cruisers, troopships, hospital ships, wartime cargo transports and so on. Most of these vessels were faster than conventional warships and had considerably more space both for passengers (troops) and cargo. Despite this suitability, however, the liners were not designed to fight at sea.

By the end of spring 1914 most American visitors to Europe had had no idea of the impending war and were completely surprised by its eventual beginnings. All over Europe many Americans were trying to book passage home at the beginning of August to avoid the looming conflagration. The demand was such that White Star Line's London office was forced to stay open later than its normal closing time of 1 p.m. on a Saturday. Most of the company's westbound vessels were fully booked, despite the fare increase due to extra insurance, whereas the eastbound sailings had plenty of room! Across the Atlantic most Americans, including ex-British and ex-German, wished to remain neutral.

A considerable number of passenger liners were rapidly withdrawn and joined the war service. Portholes were painted over, deck lights extinguished and paint liveries changed. The White Star Southampton service to New York was 'temporarily suspended'.

At the declaration of war, Australia and New Zealand both volunteered to send troops to Europe. Three White Star vessels were requisitioned and converted to troopships.

For the next four years Britain's merchant marine contributed enormously to the war effort. It is thought that over 5,000 vessels and over 15,000 lives were lost as a result of the fighting at sea. Lord Pirrie, the owner of Harland & Wolff Shipbuilders, ordered both the Belfast and Glasgow yards be enlarged to handle the ever-increasing war demands.

A number of Britain's larger vessels were considered to be somewhat unwieldy and 'too valuable to lose'. They were to have a different function not much later!

Germany decided to use their vessels on a solitary basis. However, they were restricted by their considerable coal consumption. New British builds, however, upon completion were immediately handed over to government authorities and pressed into service as troop transports, hospital ships, cargo vessels and so on.

One of Britain's first decisions was to create the 10th Cruiser Squadron, formed of a considerable number of passenger liners converted into naval auxiliaries. Immediately, construction of *Britannic* (2) ceased and *Cedric*, *Celtic* (2), *Oceanic* (2) and *Teutonic* were taken over as armed merchant cruisers. With very little, if any, armour plating and only lightly armed with elderly guns, the speed of the vessels was their real defence. The squadron, sometimes known as Cruiser Force B, and manned by the Volunteer Reserve formed mostly by the vessels' own civilian officers and crew, patrolled the North Sea blockade, covering the approaches to Europe from the North Atlantic. The squadron was terminated in December 1917.

The Dardanelles campaign had commenced in April 1915 with the invasion of the Gallipoli Peninsula by Britain and France in order to force a route through to Russia via the Bosporus. The campaign was an expensive mistake and the attack failed. Cunard's remaining large vessels, *Aquitania* and *Mauretania*, had initially been used to carry troops to the Dardanelles but, with the enormous number of casualties, were rapidly converted into hospital ships.

As the disastrous involvement in the Gallipoli campaign was drawing to a close, British shipping losses were reaching an enormous number. For example, during the period from February to September in 1915, most sinkings were as a result of torpedoes fired from German submarines, including that of the Cunard liner *Lusitania* with an appalling loss of life. Of the nearly 2,000 people on board the ship 1,198 lost their lives including 128 American citizens. According to the rules of war, submarines were to ensure that all passengers and crew of civilian vessels were safely evacuated before an attack was commenced. This became no longer possible as Allied anti-submarine measures grew.

The convoy system was not introduced by the British Admiralty until 1917. The first convoy departed the USA on 24 May 1917 and only one vessel from that convoy was lost. Prior to this the Admiralty had only issued the following directives: to avoid headlands and steer a course in mid channel; to travel at full speed near harbours and keep radio silence within 100 miles of land unless in case of emergency; to increase lookouts and have lifeboats ready for lowering; and to increase speed outside harbours and maintain a zig-zag course.

In early 1917 Germany introduced unrestricted submarine warfare. This meant that any vessel, British or neutral, could be sunk without warning, a contributory factor in bringing the United States into the war on the side of the Allies. The U-boat threat was lessened by the introduction of the convoy system as well as that of the depth charge.

The Royal Navy's blockade of Germany was beginning to threaten the German population with starvation and, with the US entry into the European theatre of war on 6 April 1917, the German army's losses were becoming desperate.

Toward the end of the war one of the measures introduced by Britain was 'Dazzle Paint Camouflage'. This was the idea of Norman Wilkinson, the marine artist who had painted the pictures in the first-class smoking room of White Star's liners *Olympic* and *Titanic*, and his team. The system was soon widely accepted as dazzle painting broke up the silhouette of a vessel, thus making it difficult for a submarine commander to estimate a ship's size or direction of travel. Initially this was so successful that the Admiralty decided that all merchant vessels should be so painted. The full success of this camouflage system may, however, not ever be truly known.

Significantly, the termination of total naval responsibility for trooping came about by the creation of the Sea Transport Section of the Ministry of Shipping in 1917, thus removing the last link with the Royal Navy. Requisitioned vessels were no longer chartered to the Admiralty as had been the case during the Boer War.

GERMAN MERCANTILE MARINE AT THE START OF THE FIRST WORLD WAR

About 12 per cent of Germany's merchant shipping was seized in British and Empire ports at the outbreak of hostilities, and the remaining ships at sea were advised to take shelter in neutral ports. Allowing for the subtraction of these vessels there remained just 2 million tons of German shipping after five months of warfare. Allowing also for the British Naval blockade, very few of these vessels would risk the move into open waters.

THE BRITISH SHIPPING CONTROLLER

This was a post created by the Coalition Government in 1916. It was the duty of the Shipping Controller to control, regulate and organise merchant shipping, following considerable losses, so that the UK could continue to be supplied with the necessary materials required to fight the war. The post was created on 10 December 1916 and the first holder was Sir Joseph Maclay. The second, and final, holder was Lord Pirrie and he held the post from 1918 until its abolition in 1921.

The Shipping Controller worked with the shipping companies in the requisition of liner services by the implementation of the Liner Requisition Scheme, details of which can be obtained from the 1917 National Archives at Kew. (These records have not been digitised and cannot be downloaded.)

3

WHITE STAR LINERS IN THE FIRST WORLD WAR

Germanic

The single screw *Germanic* (sister to *Britannic* 1) was sold by White Star after 1903, ultimately to Turkey as a troop transport and renamed *Gul Djemal* in March 1911. As such she carried Turkish troops to the Gallipoli Peninsula after the Anglo–French landings there in 1915. Torpedoed by the British submarine *E14*, it is said that over 4,000 men died, she was assisted back to Istanbul by two Bosporus ferries. Post the war she was returning 1,500 troops and their weapons to Germany when she came across the British control point. After a great deal of confusion, she was eventually allowed to continue to Germany but her troops were disarmed. She was scrapped at Messina in 1950.

Above right: Germanic: Built 1874. Gross tonnage 5,008. Cross trees on her forward mast indicate that she once had auxiliary sail power.

Below: Germanic as the Turkish 'Gulcemal': Sold to Turkey in 1910 and renamed *Gul Djemal*, thus operated by the enemy in the First World War.

Runic (1)

Sold in 1912, for the second time, and renamed *Imo*. On the way to collect relief supplies for Belgium on 6 December 1917 she collided, in Halifax harbour, with French Line's *Mont Blanc* carrying a cargo of 2,800 tons of munitions. The *Mont Blanc* blew up and disintegrated, killing at least 1,600 residents and injuring over 9,000, but the *Imo*, having lost most of her lifeboats, her funnel and two of her masts, survived the blast and drifted aground. She was repaired in 1918, sold again in 1920 and having run aground in the Falkland Islands became a total loss.

Cufic (2)

Cufic (2) and her sister *Tropic* were built as cattle/cargo carriers, the *Cufic* (2) had her name changed, from *American*, when she was acquired by IMMC in 1904. In April 1917 she was commandeered by the British Shipping Controller under the Liner Requisition Scheme.

Runic: Built 1889. Gross tonnage 4,833. Renamed *Tampican* 1895, *Imo* 1912, *Governoren* 1918.

Cufic: Built 1895. Gross tonnage 8,249. Launched as *American*, transferred and renamed in 1904.

Teutonic

In June 1907 the White Star Line decided to move their express New York service from Liverpool to Southampton. Four vessels, including the *Teutonic*, made the move thus enabling them to operate their usual Wednesday departure from the UK. She was requisitioned as an armed merchant cruiser in September 1914 in the 10th Cruiser Squadron. In August 1915 the Admiralty purchased her from White Star and armed her with 6-inch guns. Placed in reserve for nearly a year in December 1916, she trooped to Alexandria before being laid up off Cowes. She was scrapped in Emden in 1921. The *Teutonic* had been the last White Star Line vessel to hold the transatlantic speed record but after this the policy had been 'comfort, reliability and safety'.

Teutonic: Built 1889. Gross tonnage 9,984. Acquired by the Admiralty on 16 August 1915. 6-inch guns are visible on her stern.

Teutonic as an Armed Merchant Cruiser leaving Portsmouth Harbour.

Teutonic held in reserve at Southampton during 1917. Interestingly, a four-funnelled liner (right) can be seen in the distance.

Majestic (1)

After release from her Boer War duties, *Majestic* (1) returned to Belfast in 1902 for a refit. Funnels were heightened, new boilers installed, tonnage increased and masts reduced to two. She joined her sister *Teutonic*, with two other vessels, in the move to Southampton in 1907. In 1912, by this time held in reserve, she replaced the lost *Titanic* until 1914 when, in May, she arrived at Morecambe for scrapping. It seems a pity that, with war imminent in 1914, the *Majestic* was not used as an armed merchant cruiser or troopship.

Right: Majestic: Built 1890. Gross tonnage 9,965. Laid-up at Birkenhead (1911). Tonnage was increased to 10,147 after 1903 refit.

Below: Majestic in spring 1914 awaiting scrapping at Morecambe. With war only four months away, and a vital need of shipping, it seems a pity to have scrapped her.

Bovic & Naronic

Bovic and her sister *Naronic* were built for the Liverpool to New York cargo/cattle service. They could also accommodate twelve passengers each. The *Naronic* would be White Star's only vessel to go missing with all hands having departed Liverpool on 11 February 1893. From February 1914 the *Bovic* inaugurated the Manchester–New York service, and as such she had her funnel

and masts reduced in height to facilitate her passage under the bridges of the Manchester Ship Canal. In April 1917 she was commandeered for war service under the Liner Requisition Scheme and returned to White Star in 1919. Transferred to Leyland & Co. (also IMMC) and renamed *Colonian* in 1922, her masts were increased to normal height. She was scrapped in Rotterdam in 1928.

WHITE STAR LINE.
Royal & United States Mail Steamers
WEEKLY ITINERARY.

Liverpool & New York Service.
MAJESTIC—Arr. NEW YORK, 6·0 a.m.. 12th April, Passage 5 days 22 hours.
TEUTONIC—Arr. QUEENSTOWN, 10·27 a.m., 12th April.
BRITANNIC—Left QUEENSTOWN, 1·20 p.m. 13th April
GERMANIC—Left NEW YORK, 4·0 p.m., 12th April.
ADRIATIC—In DOCK, LIVERPOOL.

TEUTONIC—Leaves LIVERPOOL, 19th April.
MAJESTIC—Leaves NEW YORK, 19th April.

CARGO STEAMERS.
BOVIC—Left NEW YORK, 8 a.m., 12th April.
NARONIC—Left LIVERPOOL, 6·30 a.m. 11th Feb.
TAURIC—Left LIVERPOOL, 3·0 p.m., 7th April.
NOMADIC—In DOCK, LIVERPOOL.
RUNIC–Arr. NEW YORK, midnight, 11th April.
CUFIC—Left NEW YORK, 8·0 p.m., 4th April.

CUFIC—Leaves LIVERPOOL, 21st April.
RUNIC—Leaves NEW YORK, 18th April.

London & New Zealand Service
DORIC—Left CAPETOWN, 7th April.
IONIC—Left CAPETOWN, 6th April.
COPTIC—Left TENERIFFE, 12th April.

COPTIC—Leaves LONDON, 11th May.
DORIC—Leaves NEW ZEALAND, 13th May.

San Francisco, Japan & China Service.
BELGIC—Left YOKOHAMA, 8th April.
GAELIC—Left SAN FRANCISCO, 4th April.
OCEANIC—Arr. HONG KONG, 7th April.

BELGIC—Leaves SAN FRANCISCO, 4th May.
OCEANIC—Leaves HONG KONG, 18th April.

LIVERPOOL, 13th April, 1893.   ISMAY, IMRIE & CO.

A White Star fleet advisory sent to Leipzig from the White Star Line in Liverpool on 13 April 1893. *Naronic* was lost with all hands on that voyage.

Bovic: Built 1892. Gross tonnage 6,583. Her masts have now been raised to their original height. (Renamed *Colonian*)

Gothic/Gothland

After her repatriation service during the Boer War the *Gothic* was transferred (within IMMCo) to Red Star Line and became *Gothland*, as *Gothic* again from 1911 to 1913, she reverted to Red Star's Antwerp–New York service as *Gothland* offering a limited service from Rotterdam after the German invasion of Belgium. She was scrapped in the Firth of Forth in 1926.

Gothic: Built 1893. Gross tonnage 7,755. Alternately switched between Red and White Star lines and renamed *Gothland* under Red Star ownership.

Above: Cevic: Built 1894. Gross tonnage 8,301. Converted into dummy battle-cruiser *Queen Mary* for the first year of war.

Below left: Cevic as a dummy battle-cruiser – mostly wood and canvas!

Below right: HMS *Queen Mary*: Built 1913. The original battle-cruiser which blew up at the battle of Jutland in 1916. (Tucks Oilette)

Cevic

The *Cevic* was built to replace the lost *Naronic* and would be one of the last White Star cattle/cargo vessels. In December 1914 she was converted by Harland & Wolff, with wood and canvas, to resemble the battlecruiser HMS *Queen Mary*. One of fourteen vessels so changed, their disguise proved to be quite effective and may have resulted in the German commerce-raider *Kronprinz Wilhelm* applying for internment in New York. After the *Queen Mary* had been sunk at the Battle of Jutland in 1916, the *Cevic* was converted into an oil tanker and permanently taken over by the British government. She was scrapped at Genoa in July 1933 after three name changes.

Georgic (1)

Built in 1895, she would be one of the largest cattle/cargo vessels constructed at the time. Travelling from Philadelphia to Liverpool via Brest carrying a cargo of 10,000 barrels of oil, wheat and 1,200 horses, the vessel was stopped by the German raider *Moewe*. Little could be done to save the horses and the *Georgic* was shelled and sunk 550 miles south-east of Cape Race in December 1916.

Georgic: Built 1895. Gross tonnage 10,077. 1,200 horses drowned when she was sunk in 1916. (Nautical Photo Agency)

Canada

Built for Dominion Line's (IMMC) service from the UK to Canada. She served as a troopship throughout the First World War and is seen here in 1917 on the way to Russia. After spending the rest of her life in the Canadian service she was scrapped in Italy in August 1926.

Built 1896. Gross tonnage 8,806. As a troopship en route to Russia 1917. She was also used to accommodate POWs during the First World War. (P.A. Vicary)

Delphic (1)

Delphic carried troops to the Cape, whilst on the way to New Zealand, for the Boer War. Between the Boer War and the First World War she remained on the New Zealand service, but in 1917 she was requisitioned under the Liner Requisition Scheme and while taking a cargo of coal from Cardiff to Montevideo the vessel was torpedoed and sunk.

Delphic: Built 1897. Gross tonnage 8,273. Sunk by *UC72* in August 1917. (Nautical Photo Agency)

Cymric

For nearly ten years after her Boer War service *Cymric* remained on the Liverpool to Boston route and for two more years she returned to her New York route. In April 1916, with no passengers on board, she departed New York for Liverpool but, on 8 May, was torpedoed by *U20* and sank early the next morning, 140 miles off Fastnet with the loss of five lives.

Cymric: Built 1898. Gross tonnage 13,096. Torpedoed by *U20* that had sunk the Cunard liner *Lusitania* the previous year.

Afric

The first of five vessels built at Harland & Wolff for the service from the UK to Australia. With *Medic* and *Persic*, they each carried 320 passengers in third class. During the early years of the First World War the *Afric* continued her regular service to Australia but on the way to Sydney she was torpedoed and sunk by *UC66* off Eddystone light with the loss of twenty-two lives. She carried the pennant A19.

Afric: Built 1899. Gross tonnage 11,948. Torpedoed and sunk February 1917. (Kingsway Real Photo Service)

Medic: Built 1899. Gross tonnage 11,985. Liverpool's Liver Building is in the background.

Medic

Like her sisters *Afric* and *Persic*, *Medic* continued on her commercial service during the first years of the First World War, but in April 1917 she was taken over under the Liner Requisition Scheme for war service and was released in March 1919. She carried the pennant A7.

Oceanic

One of the largest liners in the world, her construction was supervised by the Admiralty for use as an Armed Merchant Cruiser in the event of war. *Oceanic* was one of the four vessels that White Star moved from Liverpool to Southampton to operate the New York express service in 1907.

On 8 August 1914 she was taken over by the Admiralty as an armed merchant cruiser, fitted with sixteen 4.7in guns and allocated to patrol duties with the 10th Cruiser Squadron watching for German warships or blockade runners. As such she had two captains, a Royal Navy captain, with no experience in handling such a large vessel, and her own peacetime commander with many of her crew, some of whom were also in the R.N.R. This combination led to rivalry and disagreement between the two commanding officers. Her White Star Captain had cautioned against taking such a large vessel so near the Shetland Islands and the possibility of running onto any reef.

In a flat calm sea and in good weather, on 8 September 1914, the *Oceanic* ran firmly aground on rocks 20 miles off the Shetlands. She could not be moved and, two weeks later, rough weather caused her to damage her hull to such an extent that she could not be saved. After this incident the Admiralty decided that, in future, the Royal Navy should patrol the Northern Approaches and that large merchant ships would remain

Above: Oceanic: Built 1899. Gross tonnage 17,274. She was to have a sister ship named *Olympic* but construction was abandoned.

Below: Oceanic.

under the command of their own captains. They also abolished the habit of having two men in command of any vessel.

Officer Lightoller, second officer on board RMS *Titanic* and who was serving on board *Oceanic*, said in his book, *Titanic and Other Ships*, 'The *Oceanic* was really too big for that patrol, and in consequence it was not long before she crashed onto one of the many outlying reefs and was lost.'

On 25 August 1916 an auction was held at Southampton of fixtures and fittings that had been removed from *Oceanic* in August 1914. Most of the salvage was accomplished by 1924 and the remainder of the vessel was removed by 1973.

Oceanic stranded on the rocks forever! (1914)

Persic

She maintained her commercial service until, on 9 November 1917, she was taken up under the Liner Requisition Scheme by the Shipping Controller for war service. In September 1918 she was torpedoed by *U87* off the Scilly Isles whilst carrying nearly 3,000 American soldiers. *Persic*, carrying pennant A34, made port and was beached. Released from duties in July 1919, she was scrapped in the Netherlands in July 1927.

Persic: Built 1899. Gross tonnage 11,973. Dressed overall, a rare image!

Runic (2)

She and *Suevic* were slightly larger than the three sister predecessors *Afric*, *Medic* and *Persic*. With *Suevic* she completed the White Star provision of a five-ship service to Australia. In January 1915 she became an Australian troop transport having been given the designator A54. She was taken by the Shipping Controller in November 1917 under the Liner Requisition Scheme and released back to White Star in April 1919.

Runic: Built 1900. Gross tonnage 12,482. Still a troopship in February 1920. Repatriation HMT?

Suevic 2

When the Boer War ended *Suevic*, and her sisters, remained on the service from the UK to Australia until, in March 1907, she ran aground on the Manacles Rocks near the Lizard Peninsula. It was decided to leave the bow impacted on the rocks, remove the rest of the vessel with dynamite and move it to Southampton with the aid of four tugs. A new bow was built at Harland & Wolff in Belfast, towed to Southampton and the two parts were joined up. The *Suevic* returned in January 1908 and the five ships remained on the Australian route, at the beginning of the First World War, predominantly because of their large frozen meat carrying ability. During the period between 1917 and 1919 she operated under the Liner Requisition Scheme until her release in July 1919. *Suevic* was to carry the pennant A29.

Suevic: Built 1900. Gross tonnage 12,531. The rear portion steaming astern into Southampton to await a new bow (1907).

Suevic as Troopship A29. Repaired and serving her country!

Finland

Although this vessel and her sister *Kroonland* were built for the Red Star Line in 1902, they both operated from New York to Liverpool under the management of the American Line (IMMCo) from 1916. In April 1920 both vessels resumed sailings to New York from Antwerp for the Red Star Line for three years. She was scrapped in 1927.

Finland: Built 1902. Gross tonnage 12,760. Transferred to American Line (IMMCo) in 1923. Operated New York to Hamburg.

THE 'BIG FOUR'

Celtic (2)

This vessel was not only the last ship to be ordered by Thos. Ismay but also the first ship in what was to become known as 'The Big Four'. When built she was the largest ship in the world. At the outbreak of the First World War she was immediately requisitioned as an armed merchant cruiser by the Admiralty, fitted with eight 6-inch guns and, in October, joined the 10th Cruiser Squadron. In January 1916 she was decommissioned as it was now felt that large liners were too vulnerable to be used as warships. Whilst working under the Liner Requisition Scheme she was mined in 1917 and torpedoed in 1918. Surviving both attacks she was released back to White Star in 1919. During the Great War she became the most widely travelled of the four sister ships. Sadly, in December 1928, she ran aground on rocks outside Cobh harbour and was written off as a total loss.

Above: Celtic: Built 1901. Gross tonnage 21,035. First of the 'Big Four'.

Below: Celtic at Roches Point, Cobh. Wrecked!

Cedric

Virtually identical to *Celtic*, she was the second ship of the 'Big Four' and was also converted into an armed merchant cruiser and allocated to the 10th Cruiser Squadron. Like her sister *Celtic* she was decommissioned in 1916. Before some trooping she was brought under the Liner Requisition Scheme in April 1917. Resuming her service after a refit in September 1919, she was scrapped in 1932.

W. P. HARTLEY'S AINTREE WORKS

A MOTOR Load of Hartley's Seville Oranges just leaving the docks for Hartley's Marmalade Factory. The White Star Liner "Cedric" is waiting to leave for America, and Hartley's Motors are on the way to it with several loads of Marmalade for New York.

Left: The name on *Cedric*'s bow has been moved forward, photographically, for the purposes of advertising!

Below: Cedric: Built 1903. Gross tonnage 21,035. A very popular ship. Cruised to the Mediterranean annually from 1906.

Baltic

Over 2,800 tons larger than her sisters *Celtic* and *Cedric*, the White Star Line had requested a larger vessel but not any increase in engine power. This increase in size resulted in a loss of speed which, despite modification of the engines, increased coal consumption considerably. At the outbreak of the First World War she remained on the Liverpool–New York service – in fact her arrival at New York on 22 August 1914 was with a passenger load of 2,072. Many of these were rich Americans travelling in Third Class, unable to book better due to the vast numbers escaping the war. She operated under the Liner Requisition Scheme for trooping from 1915 to the end of 1918. It was noticed in June 1916 that she had a new paint scheme. Her hull had been painted black and her superstructure a battleship grey. In 1917 she carried General Pershing, his HQ staff and the first US troops over to Europe. She was scrapped in Osaka in 1933.

24,000 TONS.   725 FT. 9 IN. LONG.   75 FT. BROAD.   49 FT. DEEP.

Above: Baltic was the third of the 'Big Four' but, although larger, she was not given the extra power.

Right: Baltic: Built 1904. Gross tonnage 23,876. A 'Ship in a Life-ring' card was popular before the First World War. This card was posted in Hoboken to Essex in May 1912.

Adriatic

Slightly larger than *Baltic* she was the largest liner in the world for half a day until the launch of Cunard's *Mauretania* in September 1906. Despite having the same dimensions as her sister ship *Baltic*, she was built with more powerful boilers thus enabling her to maintain a better speed. She was the fourth and last vessel to be transferred to Southampton from Liverpool in June 1907. The *Adriatic* was in New York at the outbreak of war and her departure was delayed by the Admiralty for several days due to the fear of German cruisers. With *Baltic*, she remained on the Liverpool–New York service. During her first westbound crossing in 1914 she carried some 2,000 Americans anxious to get home. Initially she had been armed with 6-inch guns in Liverpool but, on her return to New York, the authorities objected to the guns, stating that they were offensive, not defensive, and that they were to be removed before she returned. She coaled, left harbour on 3 September and, on her return to Liverpool, all four guns were removed and never replaced. One little-known fact is that both *Baltic* and *Adriatic* were able to carry a considerable amount of fuel-oil in their double bottoms. She was scrapped in Osaka in March 1935.

Adriatic: Built 1907. Gross tonnage 24,541. One of the first White Star liners to use Southampton. The stern portion of *Suevic* can be seen in the background (1907).

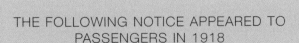

THE FOLLOWING NOTICE APPEARED TO PASSENGERS IN 1918

IMPORTANT NOTICE TO PASSENGERS ON BOARD ADRIATIC NEW YORK – LIVERPOOL 31/01/1918

Don't strike matches, smoke or use flashlamps on deck after dark. Don't take photographs, use of cameras prohibited. Don't open portholes or windows at sea. Don't switch on lights in your cabin except those actually required. Don't carry any letters or packages to or from UK or USA for posting or delivery. In the danger zone wear or carry your lifebelt; be warmly clad and be ready for any emergency. In case of accident, a general alarm will be given by five blasts on both fog whistles when you must go to your boat station; Keep calm and do what you are told by the ship's officers.

S. S. Adriatic

© Int. Film Service

Greetings from the Jewish Welfare Board to Soldiers and Sailors of the U. S. Army and Navy

America enters the war.

SHIP MOVEMENTS WITHIN THE INTERNATIONAL MERCANTILE MARINE

After J. Pierpont Morgan's International Mercantile Marine Company had absorbed the White Star Line into its fleet in 1902, there would be much transfer of vessels within the combine in 1903. Five vessels owned by IMMC companies were switched to the White Star Line and renamed. Only one, the *Republic*, was lost in 1909 through collision and did not feature in any war activity.

Cretic

Built on the Tyne for the Leyland Line, this vessel was launched as *Hanoverian* but, after only three voyages, was transferred within the IMMC to the Dominion Line in 1903 and renamed *Mayflower*. Again in 1903 she was transferred to White Star and renamed *Cretic*. Serving permanently on the Mediterranean service, she was switched to the Liner Requisition Scheme for war service duties from 1917 to 1919. During the end of this time she repatriated a considerable number of Canadian troops at Halifax. Sent back to Leyland Line in 1923, she was scrapped in 1929.

Romanic

The *Romanic* was launched for the Dominion Line as *New England* in 1898 but, in 1903, was transferred to White Star and renamed *Romanic*. In 1912 she was sold to the Allan Line and renamed *Scandinavian*. For the first two years of the First World War she would occasionally carry troops primarily from Canada until she came under the Liner Requisition Scheme for war duties. She was scrapped in Hamburg in 1923.

Above right: Cretic: Built 1902. Gross tonnage 13,507. Originally *Hanoverian*, then *Mayflower*, then *Cretic* and finally back to Leyland Line as *Devonian*!

Centre right: Romanic: Built 1898. Gross tonnage 11,394. One of the first vessels for White Star with two masts.

Below right: Romanic as Scandinavian in 1912. Her 'upper-works' look suspiciously grey!

WHITE STAR LINE, S.S. "ARABIC."   C. Scott, Photo., Liverpool

Sailed from Boston May 25th 1905.

PHOTO BY HODGE, BOSTON

"GINGER"
"S. S. ARABIC"

Our cat

Arabic (2)

Her route alternated between New York and Boston to the Mediterranean. On 19 August 1915 with 200 passengers whilst on the way to New York she was torpedoed and sunk by *U24* off the Old Head of Kinsale, the first White Star Line vessel lost in the First World War. The torpedoing had been so devastating that the *Arabic* had sunk within fifteen minutes and only excellent discipline ensured that 390 people were safely evacuated. Forty-four lives were lost, including some American citizens, and this came soon after the loss of *Lusitania* three months earlier. Three lifeboats capsized during the sinking and the survivors were rescued by patrol boats. USA attitudes were hardening against Germany to such an extent the Germans claimed the commander of the submarine believed *Arabic* was going to ram his U-boat! The Germans did agree, however, that in future submarines would give sufficient warning, prior to attack, to allow all passengers to safely disembark, a guarantee that had been in force for some time already! The ship's cat 'Ginger', a favourite amongst the passengers and crew, was sadly lost.

Far left: *Arabic*: Built 1903. Gross tonnage 15,801. The first White Star liner to be sunk in the First World War, three months after *Lusitania*.

Left: 'Ginger' on *Arabic*. So popular! It even had its own postcard!

Canopic

This vessel was launched as *Commonwealth* for the Dominion Line. She sailed as such for nearly three years before being transferred within the IMMC to White Star and renamed *Canopic*. Another two-masted vessel, the *Canopic* was to serve the Mediterranean until 1915 when her route reverted to either Boston or New York from Liverpool and then she was taken over under the Liner Requisition Scheme before her release in February 1919 and return to White Star. She was scrapped in South Wales in October 1925.

Right: *Canopic*: Built 1900. Gross tonnage 12,097. Transferred to White Star and renamed *Canopic* in 1903.

Athenic

The first of three sister vessels built for the joint service to New Zealand to be operated by White Star (supplying ships and crew) and Shaw Savill and Albion (supplying management). At the outbreak of the First World War she was retained on her commercial route owing to her high meat cargo capacity. In 1916 she changed her route to operate via the Western Hemisphere. Under the Liner Requisition Scheme, she also carried US troops on her homeward journey after the US entry into the First World War. She ran aground in the Caribbean in August 1918, in dazzle camouflage, but was later refloated. She was released back to White Star in 1919 and sold in 1928 for conversion to a whale factory ship.

Athenic: Built 1902. Gross tonnage 12,345. Her large frozen meat capacity saved her.

Left: *Athenic* ran aground for a week in the Caribbean. Onwards to New York to transport US troops.

Below: As HMNZT No.11 *Athenic* carried many New Zealand and US troops to Europe.

Corinthic in dazzle-paint camouflage but still in New Zealand service.

Corinthic

Sister to *Athenic*, she was also built for the New Zealand service. In August 1914, owing to her frozen meat capacity, she remained on her regular service. In April 1917 she took a New Zealand expeditionary force to the UK in her third-class accommodation. Even though she had been taken up under the Liner Requisition Scheme from June 1917 to 1919, she continued with her carriage of frozen meat. By July of 1921 the New Zealand ships had substituted Southampton for Plymouth both for disembarkation and embarkation. She was scrapped at Blyth in December 1931.

Corinthic: Built 1902. Gross tonnage 12,367. She carried her troops in Third Class!

Ionic: Built 1903. Gross tonnage 12,352. She carried the New Zealand Expeditionary Force to the UK in August 1914.

Ionic (2)

The third vessel of the New Zealand trio. From July 1917 to August 1919 she was taken up under the Liner Requisition Scheme and, in May 1918, trooped another division of the New Zealand expeditionary force to Europe. Released in January 1919, she continued to operate her normal service to New Zealand but via the Western Hemisphere. After the Cunard-White Star merger in 1934 the *Ionic* passed into Shaw Savill & Albion ownership. She was scrapped in Osaka 1937.

Victorian/Russian

After Boer War service, from February 1903 within IMMC she came under the management of White Star but was still owned by the Leyland Line. At the same time all passenger accommodation ceased in both her and her sister ship *Armenian* and they became cattle/cargo carriers. In 1914 she was converted into an Armed Merchant Cruiser and renamed *Russian* to avoid confusion with another vessel owned by the Allan Line. In December 1916 whilst travelling to Newport (South Wales) from Thessalonika she was torpedoed and sunk in the Mediterranean by *U43* with the loss of twenty-eight lives. (Not illustrated)

Armenian

Sister to Leyland's *Victorian* and also single-screw propulsion. Coming under White Star management, she was also converted to all cattle/cargo service in 1903. In August 1914 the *Armenian* was requisitioned as a transport for horses to France. On 28 June 1915 she was torpedoed and sunk by *U24* off the Cornish coast. She was on the way to Avonmouth with 400 mules and had been trying to escape the submarine but, after an hour, her surviving crew surrendered and, with the muleteers, abandoned ship leaving the mules to their fate. (Not illustrated)

Cufic (2) & Tropic (2)

The *Cufic* (2) had originally been named *American* when she was launched in 1895 for the West India & Pacific SS Co. and *Tropic* (2) *European* for the same company in 1896. Both vessels were used as transports during the Boer War and, in 1904, were transferred to White Star Line and renamed *Cufic* (2) and *Tropic* (2). In 1914 the *Cufic* was requisitioned by the government as a war transport and fitted with two 4.7-inch guns. *Tropic* stayed on the meat route to Australia. Both vessels were scrapped at Genoa, in 1932 and 1933 respectively. (Not illustrated)

Laurentic (1)

This vessel, and her sister *Megantic*, were built for the newly formed White Star-Dominion Line service to Canada. In conjunction with Dominion's Canada and Dominion they maintained a weekly service to Canada. In 1914 both were rapidly taken over and converted into troopships. *Laurentic* (1) was part of the 'Blue Squadron' of a thirty-two-ship convoy that took 35,000 Canadian soldiers to Europe. She left Canada on 3 October and arrived in the UK on 14 October. In 1915 she was converted into an armed merchant cruiser and fitted with 5.5-inch and 4-inch guns. In January 1917, while sailing to Canada with £5 million in gold bullion, carried to pay for munitions, the *Laurentic* (1) struck two mines laid by the German submarine *U80* off Lough Swilly. In less than an hour she had capsized and sunk in 125 feet of water. In total 354 men died, in appalling winter weather, despite the 475 aboard having mostly been able to abandon ship in lifeboats. By 1924 £4,958,000 of the gold had been recovered from the wreck. The *Laurentic* (1) would be one of the worst losses of the First World War.

Above left: *Laurentic*: Built 1909. Gross tonnage 14,892. Her propulsion system was adopted for the Olympic-class liners.

Below left: Now HMS *Laurentic*!

Megantic

Megantic joined her sister *Laurentic* (1) on the Canadian route in 1909. Both ships were nearly identical except the *Megantic* was propelled by the conventional two-propeller system whereas *Laurentic* (1) featured an additional central propeller powered by a turbine. The *Laurentic's* system proved to be the more economical and it was that which the White Star Line adopted for their new Olympic-class liners. *Megantic* joined the 'White Squadron' of the thirty-two-ship convoy departing Canada on 3 October carrying 35,000 soldiers to Europe. Having been used as a troopship in 1915, carrying 1,800 men, she was taken over under the Liner Requisition Scheme from April 1917 to December 1918. She was scrapped in Osaka in 1933.

Megantic: Built 1909. Gross tonnage 14,878. Trooping from Canada 1915.

Zeeland/Northland

Zeeland: Built 1901. Gross tonnage 11,905. After wartime closure of Red Star Line's port of Antwerp she moved to White Star Line's Liverpool-USA/Canada service.

Built by John Brown & Co. of Clydebank for the Red Star Line (IMMC) based in Antwerp. In 1910 she was switched to White Star but by 1912 was back in Antwerp. At the start of the First World War, and with the closure of the Antwerp service due to the German invasion of Belgium, she rejoined White Star to replace those vessels taken up for government service. She then formed part of the large convoy carrying Canadian troops to Europe. She was renamed *Northland* in 1915 and some believe that this was because of possible confusion with White Star's *Zealandic* of 1911 and others think that *Zeeland* sounded too Germanic! In March 1917, after seven voyages on the joint White Star–Dominion service to Canada, she was taken over by the Shipping Controller under the Liner Requisition Scheme. Released from war duty in 1919, refitted and renamed *Zeeland* in 1920 she reverted to the Red Star service from Antwerp to New York. She was scrapped at Inverkeithing in 1930.

Renamed *Northland* possibly because *Zeeland* sounded too Germanic!

Vaderland/Southland

Sister ship to the *Zeeland*, the vessel was built in 1900 also by John Brown of Clydebank. In New York when the Germans invaded Belgium, in August 1914 she made her first sailing for White Star from New York to Liverpool. In 1915 she was renamed *Southland*. Some people, again, believe that the renaming was because of the similarity to Hapag's *Vaterland* (interned in the USA) or that the name sounded too Germanic.

Taken over as a troopship in 1915 for the Dardanelles campaign she then reverted to the joint Canadian service in 1916. In April 1917, after the USA entered the war, she was used to transport American troops to Europe but, in June, on the way from Liverpool to Philadelphia was torpedoed and sunk by *U70* north-west of Tory Island, Donegal with the loss of four lives.

Vaderland/Southland: Built 1900. Gross tonnage 11,899. Once again, the renaming *Southland* might be because of the German-sounding original name.

Belgic (3)

Belgic was a ship with a very varied career. She had originally been built as the *Mississippi* for the Atlantic Transport Line (IMMC) in 1903 to carry cattle eastbound. Three years later she was switched to the Red Star Line, renamed *Samland*, and served on the Antwerp–New York run. She was transferred to White Star on 30 August 1911 and renamed *Belgic*, by which time her tonnage had increased to 10,150. In 1913 she was transferred back to Red Star and renamed *Samland*. After the German invasion of Belgium, she operated a cargo-only service from London to New York under charter to American Transport Line until February 1916. From March of that year she served the New York–Falmouth–Rotterdam route for the Belgian Relief Commission until resuming her Antwerp–New York sailings in February 1919. She was scrapped in Ghent in 1931.

Belgic: Built 1903. Gross tonnage 9,748. White Star ownership and name for only two years.

OLYMPIC

Launched at Harland & Wolff in October 1910, she was to be the first of three Olympic-class liners to be built for the White Star Line. The others were *Titanic* and *Britannic*. On 20 September 1911 an 'own goal' (militarily speaking) was scored when the R.N. cruiser HMS *Hawke* rammed the *Olympic* on her starboard rear side. The accident occurred in the Solent as *Olympic* was departing for New York. She returned to Southampton and then to Belfast for repairs which not only lasted six weeks but delayed the completion of her sister ship *Titanic*. HMS *Hawke* was torpedoed and sunk by *U9* in October 1914.

Above: Olympic: Built 1911. Gross tonnage 45,324. First of the three Olympic-class liners, the other two being *Titanic* and *Britannic*.

Below: The light cruiser HMS *Hawke* makes her way back to Portsmouth after the collision.

Above: *Olympic* is escorted back to Southampton after the collision with HMS *Hawke*.

Olympic departed Southampton on 29 July 1914 for New York. When her Captain (Haddock) learnt that war had been declared on 4 August he ordered radio silence and had all the portholes and windows blacked out. Whilst in New York her upper works and funnels were painted a dull grey. She left New York on 9 August empty of passengers and cargo and made a rapid crossing of the Atlantic to Liverpool. White Star services had discontinued from Southampton at the outbreak of war. She, with *Adriatic*, *Baltic* and *Lapland* (on loan from Red Star) continued to operate the New York express service from Liverpool.

As the White Star vessels departed New York for the UK in August 1914 they would have passed the silent crews aboard the German vessels, including the giant *Vaterland*, berthed in the New Jersey port of Hoboken across the Hudson river. Owing to the British naval blockade of their home ports they were trapped there until the US entry into the war in April 1917, at which time their ship was commandeered and used to transport troops to Europe.

Meanwhile the North German Lloyd liner *Kronprinzessin Cecilie* had left New York on 28 July on the way to Bremen. In order to escape potential British cruisers, she disguised herself as the *Olympic* by having the tops of her buff funnels painted black and sought protection in Bar Harbour, Maine. Upon the US entry into the war she was taken over and renamed USS *Mount Vernon*. North German Lloyd's vessel *Berlin* was in Germany at the outbreak of war. Rapidly taken over and converted to a minelayer, she laid a minefield in the Irish Sea then, owing to lack of fuel, she was interned at Trondheim (Norway) for the remainder of the war.

Opposite: The German liner *Kronprinzessin Cecilie* takes shelter in Bar Harbour, Maine. Loosely disguised as *Olympic*!

Untergang des englischen Grosskampfschiffes „Audacious" an der irischen Küste.

At the end of *Olympic*'s third wartime eastbound crossing, commencing 21 October 1914, she received radio warnings of the minefield in the Irish Sea. The British battleship HMS *Audacious* (23,000 gross tons) had struck one of these mines on 27 October at 8.30 a.m. and was in trouble. The *Olympic* steamed toward her and, as well as evacuating many of the seamen from *Audacious*, attempted to tow the stricken battleship. Bad weather prevented the return of *Olympic*'s lifeboats and, at 7.00 p.m. she sailed to Lough Swilly. The *Audacious* sank two hour later. *Olympic* stayed in N. Ireland for nearly a week and the Admiralty attempted to hide the loss of one of Britain's battleships by keeping *Olympic*'s passengers on board. Eventually, the minefield having been cleared, *Olympic* sailed to Belfast, her passengers disembarked and she was laid up there, with her sister *Britannic*, and withdrawn from regular service as a result of a reduction in bookings and her vulnerability. The remaining 'Big Four' vessels *Adriatic* and *Baltic* were well able to handle the express New York traffic alone from Liverpool.

Cunard Line's *Lusitania* had been lost with appalling loss of life on 7 May 1915, after which passenger service across the Atlantic virtually ceased. On 11 May Cunard's *Mauretania* and *Aquitania* were requisitioned as troopships. Not long afterwards the British Government were asking about *Olympic* and *Britannic*! They were advised by White Star that *Olympic* was available and *Britannic* would be ready within twelve weeks. *Mauretania* and *Aquitania* had both, by this time, been converted to hospital ships and therefore the British Admiralty still needed a large-capacity liner as a troopship primarily for the Dardanelles campaign. On 1 September 1915 *Olympic* was requisitioned and work began on the conversion to accommodate about 6,000 troops. The elegant and spacious parts of the vessel were transformed into sleeping and mess facilities. The first-class dining room and reception room on D deck were converted to accommodate over 3,000 men and the second-class library (reading and writing room) would now be a hospital with beds for over 100. She was armed with a 4.7-inch gun aft and forward a twelve-pounder. Having been laid up for some ten months, it was also necessary for *Olympic* to have her hull cleaned in dry dock at Liverpool. The funnels of the vessel were painted grey, leaving the black tops.

A German postcard depicting *Olympic* coming to the aid of British battleship HMS *Audacious* sinking after striking a German mine.

CANADIAN EXPEDITIONARY FORCE

CANADA TO ENGLAND, JUNE, 1916

For Peace, Justice and Freedom.   *God Save the King.*

White Star Line had wished for Captain Haddock to revert to command of *Olympic* but the Admiralty could not release him as he was still in charge of the fleet of merchant ships disguised as warships. Captain Bertram Fox Hayes arrived at Liverpool in the *Adriatic* on 16 September 1915 and assumed command of HMT *Olympic*. White Star's fee for the use of *Olympic* would be ten shillings per gross ton per month. *Olympic* then assumed her role as a troopship. She first made several unescorted voyages to Mudros during the Dardanelles and Gallipoli campaigns and then ten return voyages to Halifax taking Canadian troops to Europe. During this period the Canadian government, looking to charter vessels to transport large numbers of troops, required all ships to travel with convoy protection.

Above: Canadian troops to Europe on *Olympic*!

Below: Olympic trooping at Halifax. Her last (rear) funnel was a dummy for kitchen exhaust only.

This would have reduced *Olympic's* speed to 12 knots and she was, therefore, allowed to travel alone. After making her ten round trips to Halifax, and the supply of Canadian troops having slackened off, the *Olympic* transferred to Belfast for a refit in January 1917 where she also received six 6-inch guns with forty ratings to handle them. Later that year she sported a 'dazzle' painted camouflage designed by the naval architect Norman Wilkinson. After her refit she loaded her first US troops in New York on 25 December 1917. Whilst conveying US troops to Europe, the authorities in New York requested Captain Hays to take more troops than *Olympic* could accept in any comfort. Hays was able to persuade them that more troops would mean that those already accepted plus further additions would not arrive in any fit state!

Right: *Olympic* at Southampton in dazzle-paint camouflage. 'Cheerio' Bob was the only message on the reverse. (Real Photos (Pratt) Card)

Below: Repatriation trooping at Halifax, N.S. in 1918/19.

On 25 February 1918 the *Olympic* departed New York for Liverpool painted in the first of two dazzle camouflage schemes – large shapes and designs on her hull in shades of olive, blue and grey.

Above: A different dazzle-paint camouflage

Right: A well-known aerial view of *Olympic*. US or Canadian troops and two 6-inch guns on her stern.

On 12 May 1918, with US troops on board, *Olympic* rammed and sank German submarine *U103* off the Lizard. There were thirty-one survivors and Hays was awarded the DSC. When the vessel was being refitted in Belfast after the war a plaque was placed aboard her. It was inscribed: 'This tablet, presented by the 59th Regiment United States Infantry, commemorates the sinking of the German submarine *U103* by the Olympic on 12th May 1918, on the voyage from New York to Southampton with American troops.' It would be the only known time that a passenger liner had sunk an enemy submarine. *Olympic* had by then received another dazzle camouflage paint scheme in black, blue and blue-grey colours.

As the First World War ended on 11 November 1918, *Olympic* was chartered by the Canadian government to repatriate 5,000 Canadian troops to Halifax in December. Her repatriation of Canadian and US personnel lasted nearly a year and she arrived at Liverpool from her last duty to Halifax on 21 July 1919. During her wartime service she had carried over 80,000 Canadian and nearly 43,000 US troops across the Atlantic and nearly 25,000 soldiers to the Dardanelles. She had, deservedly, earned the nick name of 'Old Reliable'.

After five years of wartime work, it was necessary for *Olympic* to return to Belfast for a major refit in order to resume her post-war duties. During this refit she was converted from coal to oil burning. She returned to White Star's service on 25 June 1920 but operating with *Adriatic* and *Lapland* was not a great success. She needed larger running mates. In October 1935 the *Olympic* was scrapped on the Tyne and, in September 1937, her hull was taken to Thos. W. Ward's yard at Inverkeithing for final breaking up.

Above left: Repatriating Canadian troops at Halifax, N.S. in 1918.

Below left: *Olympic* on the way to the breakers yard. (Photograph J.M.P. Hooley)

Nomadic (2)

One of two tenders built by White Star Line to service their Olympic-class liners at Cherbourg. She was the largest of the two and was built to accommodate up to 1,200 passengers plus their baggage. During the Great War she was employed as a naval tender at Brest, and in 1927 she, and her sister *Traffic*, were sold, retaining their names and now serving all shipping companies. In 1934 she was renamed *Ingenieur Minard* and used on many other duties as well as tendering. On the German invasion of France, she assisted in the evacuation of British troops from Le Havre and, from 1940 to 1945 served the Royal Navy mostly on the south coast as a minelayer. Returning to Cherbourg after the Second World War, she is now on display at the Harland & Wolff yard in Belfast as the last White Star Line vessel to be built there.

Nomadic: Built 1911. Gross tonnage 1,273. Now a museum vessel at Harland & Wolff, Belfast.

Traffic (2)

The second of the two tenders built to serve the Olympic-class liners. She was considerably smaller than her sister and it was intended that she provide backup support carrying mostly third-class passengers and baggage. During the First World War she served with *Nomadic* at Brest and was sold in 1927 and again in 1934. She was renamed *Ingenieur Riebell* in 1934 and requisitioned as a minelayer (X23) by the French Navy at the start of the Second World War but was scuttled in June 1940 when Germany invaded. Raised by the Germans, she was employed by them in naval service until she succumbed to a British torpedo, on 17 January 1941, in the English Channel.

Traffic: Built 1911. Gross tonnage 675. Sunk by the British in the Second World War.

Nomadic and *Traffic* at Brest repatriating US troops on
6 October 1919. (Private Collection)

Zealandic

The last White Star ship to serve the joint service with Shaw Savill & Albion to New Zealand. Despite being taken over by the Shipping Controller, on the Liner Requisition Scheme, in July 1917 she stayed on the New Zealand service, owing to her large refrigeration space, and was released in June 1919. In September 1939, after three changes of ownership and for six years being renamed *Mamilius*, as the Furness Withy *Mamari* she was sold to the Admiralty for whom she was converted into a dummy of the small aircraft carrier HMS *Hermes*. The real HMS *Hermes* was sunk in the Indian ocean in April 1941.

Right: *Zealandic*: Built 1911. Gross tonnage 8,090. After the loss of HMS *Hermes* she was on her way to being re-converted to a cargo ship when she was beached and later torpedoed by German E-boats in 1941.

Below: HMS *Hermes*. A light aircraft carrier sunk in the Indian Ocean by Japanese aircraft.

Ceramic

The *Ceramic* remained coal powered for her whole life. As troopship A40, she carried the Australian Expeditionary Force to the UK in August 1914. She was taken up under the Liner Requisition Scheme in 1917 but, owing to her large refrigerated cargo capacity, maintained the service to Australasia. Released back to White Star in 1919 she returned to Harland & Wolff for a well-earned refit, following which she returned to her Liverpool–Sydney service.

Right: *Ceramic*: Built 1913. Gross tonnage 18,495. Largest vessel on the Australasian route until 1923. (B. & A. Feilden, Liverpool)

Lapland

Built for Red Star Line's service from Antwerp to New York, this vessel took part in the large convoy from Canada, in October 1914, taking the first contingent of Canadian troops to Europe. That same month, after the German invasion of Belgium, with the *Zeeland* and *Vaderland* she was transferred, within IMMC, to White Star's service to New York from Liverpool. Serving as a troopship under the Liner Requisition Scheme from April 1917 she was released in November 1918 and again served White Star's New York service from Liverpool and Southampton until *Olympic* was released from her repatriation duties and refit in January 1920. She then reverted to Red Star but, as a result of US immigration quotas, her third-class accommodation was reduced from 1,500 to 540. She was scrapped in Japan in 1934.

Above right: *Lapland*: Built 1909. Gross tonnage 18,695. Red Star Line but transferred to White Star during German occupation of Antwerp in the First World War.

Below right: *Lapland* in dazzle-paint camouflage.

Britannic (2)

The third ship of White Star's trio of Olympic-class liners, the other two being *Olympic* and *Titanic*. The construction of this vessel was halted twice until she was completed in 1915 as a hospital ship. The first delay was to incorporate greater life-saving facilities after the enquiries into the loss of her sister ship *Titanic* were over and the second was caused by the declaration of war in 1914. As a result, the *Britannic* would be a little larger and longer than *Olympic* and *Titanic*. Her builders, Harland & Wolff, were faced with prioritisation of Admiralty commitments and were having difficulties in finding materials.

After a period of lay-up, it was decided that she would be requisitioned as a hospital ship and was converted with 3,300 beds, a total of about 500 medical staff and a crew of about 700. As well as about fifty-five lifeboats, *Britannic* carried a sizeable number of floats each having a capacity of twenty-five. As a hospital ship, she could, at times, be carrying nearly 4,500 persons. Her completion had been within the four-week estimate by three days. White Star was paid over £76,000 by the Admiralty. She was completed and handed over in December 1915 to join Cunard's *Mauretania* and *Aquitania*.

Britannic: Built 1915. Gross tonnage 48,158. Prior to launch.

Left: *Britannic* converted into Hospital Ship during fitting out.

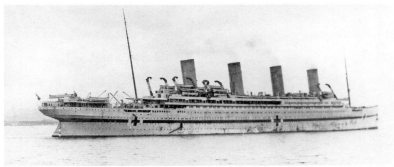

Below left: *Britannic* on duty as hospital ship. (Nautical Photo Agency)

Below right: Photo of *Britannic* taken from battleship HMS *Lord Nelson* at Mudros.

Her sister *Olympic* departed Southampton for Mudros on another trooping voyage, in February 1915. *Britannic* was left alone: this would be the last time that the two surviving sisters would be together.

Having made five return voyages to Mudros, on the Greek island of Lemnos, she was returning, mercifully empty, to collect further wounded when she struck a mine at 8.12 a.m., laid by *U73*, in the Zea Channel, south-east of Athens, in the Aegean Sea on 21 November 1916. The explosion caused damage to some of the watertight doors and a considerable number of portholes had been left open by the medical staff to air the vessel. This resulted in the *Britannic* sinking, less than an hour after striking the mine, despite all the lessons learnt from the *Titanic* enquiries. Thirty-four people lost their lives in the sinking, mostly from the still revolving propellers coming out of the sea and destroying two of the lifeboats. White Star Line now had only *Olympic* remaining of her three giant liners.

To this date the loss of *Britannic* remains the largest ever loss of a vessel in wartime. Nearly £2 million was paid to White Star by the Admiralty. Many of her luxurious furnishings were sold at auction in Belfast in July 1919.

Belgic (4)

Launched on 31 December 1914 as the *Belgenland* for Red Star Line at Harland & Wolff, she lay incomplete for nearly two and a half years until in 1917 she was given over to White Star and renamed *Belgic*. The urgent need for merchant shipping required that she be converted into a cargo vessel, also in dazzle-paint camouflage. With two funnels she also, probably amongst the first Harland & Wolff vessels, had a cruiser rather than the usual counter stern. Having been transferred by IMMC she was taken over by the Shipping Controller and served the Liverpool–New York route until 1919 when, now in Red Star Line colours, she began repatriating US troops. During 1921 she was laid up in Liverpool and in 1922 rebuilt to her original design as a passenger liner with three funnels and two masts, converted to oil-burning and renamed *Belgenland*. The rebuild increased her gross tonnage to 27,132 from 24,547. With *Zeeland* and *Lapland*, she maintained the Red Star Line service from Antwerp to New York until 1935 when she was sold and renamed *Columbia*. She was scrapped in 1936 in Firth of Forth.

Above: Belgic as Belgenland. Built 1923. Gross tonnage 27,132. Delivered to Red Star. Three black funnels with broad white bands.

Below: Belgic: Built 1917. Gross tonnage 24,547. As delivered, initially as a cargo vessel in dazzle-paint camouflage, June 1917.

Belgic with camouflage gone. Now in Red Star Line livery, 1919.

Justicia

Built at Harland & Wolff for Holland-America Line's service to New York, she was then laid up pending decision as to her future. In 1915 the British Government, after the loss of *Lusitania*, offered to buy the ship from Holland-America for £1 million but they refused the offer and instead suggested a charter for the duration of the First World War. Her name was changed to *Justicia*, from *Statendam*, in April 1917 but although she had been intended for Cunard, to replace *Lusitania*, a crew was not available, hence she was managed by White Star which, by this time, had the crew from HMHS *Britannic* ready and waiting. Before 1917 most British vessels were painted grey but, early in 1918, the *Justicia* received a dazzle-paint camouflage. In the afternoon of 19 July while in convoy from Liverpool to New York with seven other vessels and two destroyers, she fell victim to her first submarine attack. Torpedoed by *U64* off Skerryvore, Scotland, with the loss of sixteen lives, she was taken in tow towards Lough Swilly by tugs but the next day she was again attacked by submarine. This time *U124* hit her with two torpedoes and she sank at 12.40 p.m. *U124* was sunk by a British destroyer later that day. Holland-America Line was given 60,000 tons of steel by the Admiralty to compensate them for her loss.

Justicia: Built 1917. Gross tonnage 32,234. She took quite a punishment before finally sinking.

The Two Largest Vessels in the World.

MAURETANIA

R.M.S. "Mauretania,"
New Quadruple Turbine.

32,600 Tons; 68,000 H.P.;
Service Speed 25 Knots;
Length 790 ft.; Breadth 88 ft;
Depth 60½ ft.

R.M.S. "Lusitania,"
New Quadruple Turbine.

32,000 Tons; 68,000 H.P.;
Service Speed 25 Knots;
Length 787 ft.; Breadth 88 ft.;
Depth 60 ft.

LUSITANIA

F.G.O. Stuart. 1811   White Star Line R. M. S. Olympic

F.G.O. Stuart. 842   White Star Line R. M. S. Olympic

Top left: Mauretania and *Lusitania*: 'The Largest Vessels in the World'. After the construction of these two vessels was broadcast in 1906, the competitive White Star Line would later announce the construction of even larger vessels: *Olympic* and *Titanic!*

Above left: The message on the reverse of this card reads: 'Sailed for Suvla Bay. 25th September 1915'. There is no postmark, signature or addressee!

Right: Olympic. The message on the reverse of this card reads: 'Dear J. Aboard the vessel shown over-leaf – a big vessel. Very windy down here today. Hope you got my card of London. Alan'. The card was posted to Scotland from Southampton and is dated and postmarked 16 February 1916.

WOVEN IN SILK

H.M.T. NORTHLAND

HMT *Northland*. The message on the reverse of this card reads 'Dear E. Am on board, looks a nice boat, give my love to all at home. Hope to see you all again someday. Goodbye your loving brother Jack x' The card is dated 28 October 1915 and postmarked 29 October 1915. Sent to Basingstoke from Devonport. Silk postcards were very popular in the UK up to, and including, the First World War.

R.M.S. Britannic

Length, 900 ft.
Breadth, 94 ft.
Tonnage, 50,000

Britannic (2). A beautiful card depicting how the Hospital Ship *Britannic* would have looked in peacetime colours. She was completed at the beginning of the First World War and immediately fitted out as a hospital ship. Sunk, after striking a mine in 1916, she never sailed as a passenger liner.

HAMBURG-HAFEN. Großer Krahn bei Blohm und Voss.

Norddeutscher Lloyddampfer „Columbus"
Der größte Dampfer der Deutschen Handelsflotte.

Left: Majestic (2). A colour illustration of the liner *Bismarck* at the Blohm & Voss shipyard at Hamburg. She had lain incomplete throughout the First World War and, later, the Germans were obliged to complete her and, under the terms of the Treaty of Versailles, hand her over to Britain as war reparations to become White Star Line's *Majestic*.

Right: After the *Homeric*'s departure to Britain, as the German liner *Columbus*, in war reparations. The Germans were allowed to keep her sister ship *Hindenburg*, which they renamed *Columbus*. She was scuttled by her crew in the Caribbean to avoid capture by British warships during the Second World War.

Left: The White Star liner *Oceanic* aground on 8 September 1914 near the Shetland Islands. The fog has just started to lift. Two weeks later rough weather caused her wreck to be written off as a total loss. After this incident the Admiralty decided that the practice of having two captains, R.N. and mercantile marine, would be discontinued. (Original painting by Neil Egginton)

Below left: In January 1922, the White Star Line produced the above postcard outlining their post-war fleet to include the ex-German liners *Bismarck* and *Columbus* which were to become *Majestic* and *Homeric*, respectively.

Below centre: White Star Line: War Record. A twelve-page pamphlet produced by The White Star Line in 1919. (See Chapter 4)

Below right: First Class breakfast menu from maiden voyage of RMS *Majestic*.

Reprinted from *The Journal of Commerce*, Jan. 11, 1922.

WHITE STAR LINE SERVICES.

Important Developments in the Spring.

Important developments in the **White Star Line's** services will take place in the coming spring, when two great new ships, with a combined gross register of 91,000 tons, will be added to the sailings between Southampton, Cherbourg and New York, making a total in that service of 137,000 tons. The new ships are the **Majestic**, 56,000 tons, the largest steamer in the world, and the **Homeric**, 35,000 tons, the largest twin-screw steamer, and they will co-operate with the **Olympic**, 46,439 tons, the largest triple-screw steamer in the world, already well known in that service, and the trio thus formed will provide a service of unrivalled efficiency.

The **Adriatic**, 24,541 tons, will be transferred to Liverpool, where she will be operated with the **Baltic**, 23,876 tons, the **Cedric**, 21,073 tons, and the **Celtic**, 21,026 tons, in a weekly service to New York, via Queenstown. Thus the famous "Big Four" of the White Star fleet will once more operate in their original trade. The combined gross register of the steamers named, the smallest of which is over 21,000 tons, amounts to no less than 228,000 tons.

The **Pittsburgh**, a new oil-burning vessel of 16,600 tons, is nearing completion, and is destined to ply between Liverpool, Queenstown and Philadelphia, in which service she will join the **Haverford**, 11,635 tons, in the coming season. These two vessels are both of the "two class" type, which has lately become so popular with the travelling public.

The **Regina** and **Doric**, two fine steamers each over 16,000 tons gross register, are completing for the White Star-Dominion service, in which they will co-operate with the **Megantic**, 14,876 tons, the **Canada**, 9,472 tons, and the **Vedic** and **Rimouski** (the "Democratic Ships" carrying only third class), each with a tonnage of 9,300. These six ships will provide a splendid service between this country and Canada.

The total tonnage employed in the **White Star Line's** North Atlantic passenger service between England and America will then be more than **330,000** and the average tonnage of the 15 ships mentioned above is over **22,000**.

WHITE STAR LINE.

WAR RECORD.

The very necessary precaution of secrecy entailed by War conditions having now been removed, a brief account of the part played by the WHITE STAR LINE and its personnel during the world-wide conflict will, doubtless, prove of general interest; and a few facts will exemplify the ceaseless and untiring efforts made not only to co-operate with the Naval and Military Authorities in the more apparent necessities demanded by the grim struggle from which the British Empire and its heroic Allies have triumphantly emerged, but also in economic measures of scarcely less importance to the national life.

Losses in ships from enemy action have unfortunately been heavy, as a perusal of the following list will show; but they constitute the best testimony to the continued activity of the White Star Line fleet in many waters throughout hostilities.

STEAMERS LOST DURING WAR.

"BRITANNIC,"	Triple-Screw	...	48,158 tons gross register.
"OCEANIC,"	Twin-Screw	...	17,274 " "
"ARABIC,"		...	15,801 " "
"LAURENTIC,"	Triple-Screw	...	14,892 " "
"CYMRIC"	Twin-Screw	...	13,370 " "
"AFRIC,"	" "	...	11,999 " "
"GEORGIC,"	" "	...	10,077 " "
"CEVIC,"	" "	...	8,301 " "
"DELPHIC,"	" "	...	8,273 " "
		Total	148,145 " "

MAY 11TH, 1922.

R.M.S. "MAJESTIC".

⚓ Breakfast ⚓

Grape Fruit   Baked Apples
Compote of Prunes   Stewed Figs

Rolled Oats   Boiled Hominy
Puffed Rice   Shredded Wheat   Triscuit   Force

Fried Lemon Sole —— Finnan Haddie

Lamb Kidneys, Maitre d'Hotel
Split Cambridge Sausage on Toast   Minced Collops

Grilled Wiltshire Ham and Bacon

Eggs :—Fried, Turned, Poached and Hollande
Omelettes, Plain and Clamart

Cold: Roast Beef   Ox Tongue

Radishes —— Watercress

French and Graham Rolls
Cottage Loaves   Pulled Bread   Scones
Sally Lunns   Buckwheat Cakes

Conserve   Honey   Marmalade

Tea   Coffee   Cocoa   Chocolate

Britannic (2), third of White Star's Olympic-class liners, as a hospital ship. Completed and handed over to the British government by Harland & Wolff in December 1915. She never sailed as a passenger liner. (Original paining by Neil Egginton. Courtesy of Neil Egginton and Bruce Chin)

HMHS *Britannic* (2) sinking after striking a mine, laid by *U73*, in the Aegean Sea at 8.12 a.m. on 21 November 1916. Less than an hour later she had gone! (Original painting by Neil Egginton)

Neil Egginton 2016 ©

The White Star-Dominion liner HMS *Laurentic*, off Lough Swilly on 25 January 1917, sinking by the stern after striking two mines laid by *U80*. One of the worst losses of the First World War. (Original painting by Neil Egginton)

White Star's *Olympic*, carrying US troops to Europe on 12 May 1918, about to ram and sink German submarine *U103* off the Lizard – the only known time that a passenger liner had sunk an enemy submarine. There were thirty-one survivors. (Original painting by Neil Egginton)

Vedic

The *Vedic* was launched at the Govan yards of Harland & Wolff and planned initially as an emigrant carrier. After her launch in December 1917 she was moved to Belfast and completed as a cargo/troop ship. Upon completion she was taken over, briefly, under the Liner Requisition Scheme until being purchased by White Star and initially sailing from Glasgow to Boston in December 1918. Taking up to 1,250 passengers in Third Class only, she continued on the transatlantic service from Liverpool up to 1925 when she reverted to the migrant service to Australia for five years. In February 1930 she was laid up at Milford Haven until being scrapped at Rosyth in July 1934.

Haverford

One of the few vessels not built by Harland & Wolff in their yards at Belfast. This ship was launched in 1901 at John Brown & Co. yards on Clydebank for the American Line's transatlantic service. She carried troops to Mudros to fight in the Dardanelles campaign and, after the end of the First World War when she spent 1918 repatriating American troops, she was transferred within IMMC to White Star in 1921. After only three years of transatlantic service she was sold for scrap in December 1924.

Poland

Launched as the Victoria, for the Wilson's & Furness-Leyland Line joint service, at the yards of Furness Withy & Co. in West Hartlepool. Having been bought by IMMC, this vessel served the Antwerp–Philadelphia route for the Red Star Line. Continuing this service, but from Liverpool after the German invasion of Belgium, she was eventually transferred to White Star in April 1922. After only three return voyages she was scrapped in Italy in 1925.

Top right: Vedic: Built 1918. Gross tonnage 9,302. A 'one-off' to fill a post-war gap in White Star's services.

Centre right: Haverford: Built 1901. Gross tonnage 11,635. Although built for the American Line, she served Britain well during the First World War.

Bottom right: Poland: Built 1898. Gross tonnage 8,282. A varied career!

Regina

One of three liners ordered by IMMC, the others being *Pittsburgh* and *Doric*. The *Regina*, despite having been laid down in 1913 for the Dominion Line joint service to Canada, was launched in April 1917 and completed as a single-funnelled troopship with limited passenger accommodation.

Calgaric

Having been laid down for the Pacific Steam Navigation Co. in 1914 at Harland & Wolff in Belfast, work was temporarily ceased in 1916. She was launched as the *Orca* and handed over to the Shipping Controller with no passenger accommodation in 1918. The vessel was camouflaged by dazzle paint until her return to Harland & Wolff for completion to her original design. She was sold to White Star, with the *Ohio/Albertic* early in 1927 and renamed *Calgaric*. After the merger of White Star with Cunard at the end of 1934 she was scrapped at Inverkeithing in 1936.

Regina: Built 1918. Gross tonnage 16,313. Completed with single funnel and some passenger accommodation.

Calgaric: Built 1918. Gross tonnage 16,063. Completed initially as a cargo-only vessel. Gross tonnage 15,120.

THE END OF THE FIRST WORLD WAR

After the armistice in November 1918 the White Star Line had to replace many of their ships. They had lost thirteen vessels which included the third of their Olympic class, *Britannic*. The USA to Mediterranean service was resumed in July 1919 with *Canopic* and *Cretic*. Repatriation duties kept many merchant vessels in the service of their country but they no longer had to put up with the dangers of an enemy attack and, eventually, they were able to return to their peacetime duties. Throughout the First World War the White Star Line had maintained an irregular, but dangerous, passenger service between the UK and the USA. *Cedric* and *Adriatic* were the first to operate a transatlantic service followed four days later by *Baltic* and *Celtic*. It was not until November 1919 that the company's first sailing schedules were released without wartime restrictions. Services from Southampton would not restart until the summer of 1920.

4

WHITE STAR'S CONTRIBUTION

In 1919, at the cessation of hostilities, the White Star Line issued a twelve-page pamphlet detailing their contribution to the nation's struggle over the previous five years. Apart from pages 10–12, which list routes, company offices and agent's offices, the content is shown below.

WHITE STAR LINE WAR RECORD

The very necessary precaution of secrecy entailed by War conditions having now been removed, a brief account of the part played by the WHITE STAR LINE and its personnel during the world-wide conflict will, doubtless, prove of general interest; and a few facts will exemplify the ceaseless and untiring efforts made not only to co-operate with the Naval and Military Authorities in the more apparent necessities demanded by the grim struggle from which the British Empire and its heroic Allies have triumphantly emerged, but also in economic measures of scarcely less importance to the national life.

Losses in ships from enemy action have unfortunately been heavy, as a perusal of the following list will show; but they constitute the best testimony to the continued activity of the White Star Line fleet in many waters throughout hostilities.

Steamers Lost During War

"BRITANNIC,"	Triple-Screw	48,158	tons gross register
"OCEANIC,"	Twin-Screw	17,274	tons gross register
"ARABIC,"	Twin-Screw	15,801	tons gross register
"LAURENTIC,"	Triple-Screw	14,892	tons gross register
"CYMRIC"	Twin-Screw	13,370	tons gross register
"AFRIC,"	Twin-Screw	11,999	tons gross register
"GEORGIC,"	Twin-Screw	10,077	tons gross register
"CEVIC,"	Twin-Screw	8,301	tons gross register
"DELPHIC,"	Twin-Screw	8,273	tons gross register
Total	**148,145**	**tons gross register**	

On the other hand it should be mentioned that the "Vedic," a twin-screw passenger and cargo steamer of 9,332 tons gross register, was placed in commission some little time ago, and did valuable work in the latter stages of the War.

Shortly after hostilities commenced in August, 1914, the Government, recognising the suitability of high-class ocean steamers of good speed for the onerous duties of policing the great trade routes, requisitioned the services of the "Oceanic," "Teutonic," "Cedric," "Celtic," and "Laurentic," as armed cruisers, all of which maintained on War service the reputation that had made them renowned among Transatlantic travellers in days of peace. The "Oceanic," unhappily, was lost towards the end of 1914; the "Laurentic," after achieving results worthy of one of the largest and finest steamers in the Canadian trade, met her fate through submarine attack off the coast of Ireland in January, 1917; whilst the "Teutonic," the first British mercantile armed cruiser, and the product of the late Mr. T. H. Ismay's far sighted and patriotic policy, after constant duty in the North Sea Patrol has been acquired by the Government and is still in Admiralty Service. The sister-ships, "Cedric" and "Celtic", remain, and are once again employed in the Company's Liverpool and New York Passenger service, and with the "Adriatic" and "Baltic," are among the most attractive steamers in the New York trade. The aggregate gross register of these four famous liners alone is 90,000 tons.

It is greatly to be deplored that the magnificent new triple-screw steamer "Britannic," 48,158 tons gross register, for which as successful a career in the Transatlantic trade might reasonably have been anticipated as was enjoyed by the first famous vessel of the name, was sunk either by submarine or mine in the Aegean Sea on November 21st, 1916, when engaged in the humanitarian role of a hospital ship. Her whole career, indeed, had been so occupied. On her first voyage she went to Mudros and brought back 3,300 sick and wounded to Southampton. On the next three voyages the "Britannic" called at a Mediterranean port, and there the wounded for England were transferred to her from vessels that had brought them from Mudros. The fifth was her last voyage. Bound on the same errand of mercy, the "Britannic's" but patriotic career was terminated as mentioned, either by submarine or mine in the Aegean Sea; but not before she had restored nearly 15,000 disabled heroes to the homeland, amid the surroundings of the most perfectly appointed hospital ship of the War. Not only was there an operating theatre on board, but also two X-Ray Rooms of the latest type, and special apartments for mental cases. The "Britannic," in fact, was provided with every known equipment for the alleviation of human suffering.

But it is the "Olympic," the ship that has made history, that calls for special mention. And this for many reasons. The largest British steamer, it may, without presumption, be claimed that the "Olympic's" career throughout the War was one of such conspicuous merit as to entitle her, amongst many gallant rivals, to the honour of the first place in the esteem and admiration of the British people for its Mercantile Marine. Who, now, has not heard of the "Audacious" and of the rescue of her crew by the "Olympic" – a stirring deed, and one that earned a letter of appreciation and thanks from Admiral Jellicoe to the Directors of the Line. And then her later services in many waters; how during the Gallipoli campaign she carried as many as 8,000 troops on one occasion; next brought Canadian soldiers and Chinese labour battalions in vast numbers voyage by voyage across the Atlantic; and when our American kinsmen joined the Allies, had the honour of bringing these warriors in thousands to Europe. Much more might be written of the "Olympic", but here suffice a brief allusion to one of her encounters with submarines. In the darkness of an early morning in May last year, when the good ship with her precious freight was nearing the entrance to the English Channel, the man on the look-out detected a submarine on the surface. At once one of the forward guns blazed out, and, with her helm hard over, the mighty "Olympic" swung round and crashed full speed into the enemy, then pursued her way contentedly whilst a destroyer in the escort remained to rescue some 31 survivors of the submarine's crew of 60. Said a leading London daily paper a little time ago:-

"She has carried well over 200,000 people while on War service, including hundreds of women and children, wives and families of Canadian soldiers returning to Canada, and she has also been the favourite ship for most of the notable people who have crossed the Atlantic on National business during the War."

The "favourite ship," it should be added, steamed some 184,000 miles in her War career and consumed 347,000 tons of coal, her engines working perfectly throughout the whole period – a marvellous feat.

Reference may be made fitly also to the services rendered by the Australian steamers of the White Star Line. Six of these, "Ceramic," – the largest vessel in the Australian trade – "Suevic," "Runic," "Persic," "Afric," and "Medic" all noted as carrying one class of passenger only in pre-War days, were promptly requisitioned by the Australian Government, and for over four years were employed in conveying troops from the Antipodes to the Mother Country. Of a total number of 112,000 so carried, the "Ceramic" took as many as 3,000 soldiers on one trip. These same ships are now engaged in the repatriation of Australasian troops and dependents. In all, the enormous number of over a half a million troops was carried by the Company's vessels in the epoch-making four years of conflict.

How far-spread were the operations of the White Star Line steamers in the World War may be gauged by an allusion to some of their destinations which comprised, in addition to the ordinary routes, the Falkland Islands, Pacific Ocean *via* the Straits of Magellan, Panama Canal, Newport News, Newfoundland, Nova Scotia, Cape Breton, Mudros, Bombay, Colombo, Karachi, East and West Coast of Africa, etc. One vessel sailed from Liverpool to the Persian Gulf *via* the Mediterranean, thence to Australia, and returned to the Mersey *via* the Cape of Good Hope, a voyage of 25,544 miles; more than one left Liverpool for Australia and returned to the home port *via* the Panama Canal; and the "Laurentic" was away from Liverpool for the lengthy period of 21 months in continuous Admiralty service.

It was generally recognised, once the Germans had begun their inhuman submarine campaign against all shipping, that the greatest danger to this country lay in the direction of food shortage. It is obvious that, whatever the prowess of our Army and Navy, their efforts would have been brought to nought had starvation overtaken the land. And so the great cargo carriers of the White Star Line – which has for decades past been ever to the fore in Trans-Atlantic freight traffic – should be paid a tribute of gratitude in that these steamers, despite every atrocity that could be devised by a cruel and unscrupulous foe, continued undauntedly to cross the Ocean, their holds full of grain and produce by which the people of these Islands might live. No fanciful tale, this, as figures will prove, for throughout the War the Company's steamers have carried the vast total of 4,250,000 tons of cargo.

Here, also, may be narrated how the White Star Line helped to solve a difficult problem for the Navy. Over two years ago, owing to the loss of so many tank ships by enemy action, our naval oil-burning vessels were in difficulties for fuel, and immediate steps were necessary to ensure the continued supply of oil. This Company was able to assist in overcoming any cause for anxiety by arranging to carry oil in the deep tanks of the four steamers "Adriatic," "Baltic," "Cedric," and "Celtic"; and the "Celtic" left New York on August 8th, 1917, with oil in her deep tanks, this being the first consignment so carried in any passenger steamer. The experiment proved entirely successful. Some 2,500 to 3,500 tons were taken every voyage by each of the steamers named until the end of last year – a total of 88,000 tons; and the White Star Line received the cordial thanks of the Admiralty for what it had gladly been able to do in this connection.

So much for military and economic features. But something should be said also of the War deeds of those serving the White Star Line in many capacities both ashore and afloat. The Elizabethan age is usually considered the golden era of English courage and English resourcefulness; but it may be doubted if the most heroic acts of the far-famed gentlemen adventurers of Devon exceeded in valour what was done the past four years by that splendid body of men constituting the British Mercantile Marine. In whatever capacity they served their Country they covered themselves with abiding honour. No fewer than 325 officers, engineers, pursers, and surgeons of the White Star Line were attached to the Navy during hostilities, and the distinctions gained by them were many; whilst it is gratifying to add that the achievements of the men who continued in the less conspicuous but equally dangerous duties of the Merchant Service received their due reward from the Government. And it is a proud opportunity to say that the lower ratings are as justly entitled to a meed of praise as those of the upper deck; for by their unflinching courage and resolution throughout the struggle they maintained the unsullied prestige inherited from former generations of British seamen. Hardly an action of note on the sea in which some White Star men did not participate – Coronel, Falkland Islands, Jutland, Zeebrugge, to name those that come foremost to memory – and whether their lot brought them to work with the Dover Patrol, or in the bleak Russian waters, or in the Indian Ocean, in every instance the honour of the Empire did not suffer at their hands. And so with those of the clerical staff who joined the sister service, not a few of whom will return no more. It would be invidious to mention names, but the following particulars of decorations gained tell their own tale:-

2 A.D.C. to H.M. THE KING

1 C.B.	12 D.S.O.	4 M.M.
1 C.M.G.	2 D.S.C.	2 D.C.M.
10 O.B.E.	3 M.C.	1 M.S.M.

With the War and its necessities behind us, every effort will now be made by the White Star Line to maintain its popularity with ocean travellers by a continuance of careful and vigilant attention to their needs. In this year of Peace the Company, by a happy coincidence, celebrates its Jubilee, having been founded in 1869; and under such auspices the future will be faced with confidence.

White Star Line Fleet
Gross Tonnage

OLYMPIC	46,359		
ADRIATIC	24,541		
BALTIC	23,876		
CEDRIC	21,039		
CELTIC	20,904		
CERAMIC	18,481		
MEGANTIC	14,878		
CRETIC	13,518		
SUEVIC	12,531		
RUNIC	12,489		
ATHENIC	12,345		
CORINTHIC	12,343		
IONIC	12,332		
CANOPIC	12,097		
PERSIC	12,042		
MEDIC	12,032		
VEDIC	9,332		
CUFIC	8,249		
TROPIC	8,230		
ZEALANDIC	8,090		
BARDIC	8,010		
GALLIC	7,912		
BOVIC	6,583		
NOMADIC (Tender)	1,260		
TRAFFIC (Tender)	640	BUILDING	
MAGNETIC (Tender)	619	HOMERIC	33,600
PONTIC (Tender)	395	STEAMER	16,000
		ADDITIONAL	
TOTAL	**341,127**	TONNAGE	49,600

AN EXCERPT FROM SIR BERTRAM HAYES BOOK *HULL DOWN*, PUBLISHED BY MACMILLAN IN 1925, DESCRIBING *OLYMPIC'S* ARRIVAL IN HALIFAX WITH RETURNING CANADIANS IN 1919

It seemed only natural to us that the first of the victorious troops we were to take back to their homeland should be Canadians.

The reception they met with on their arrival at Halifax I will never forget. The scene was simply indescribable. Every ship in the harbour, moving or stationery, was decked with flags and every one of them kept their whistles blowing all the time we were in sight of them. The ends of the piers we passed on our way uptown were crowded with people who added to the noise by their shouts of welcome. Banners of welcome were stretched along the sheds, and perhaps what touched me most was that our ship was not forgotten in the general welcome to the troops. 'Welcome to the Old Reliable' was prominently displayed.

THE TREATY OF VERSAILLES (28 JUNE 1919)

The Treaty was signed in Versailles exactly five years after the assassination of Archduke Franz Ferdinand which had led directly to the First World War. The Treaty required Germany to disarm, make territorial concessions and pay reparations to countries that had formed the Allied powers.

Peace Treaty of Versailles (Reparations) Annex 111

Paragraph 1. Germany recognizes the right of the Allied and Associated Powers to the replacement, ton for ton (gross tonnage) and class for class, of all merchant ships and fishing boats lost or damaged owing to the war. Nevertheless, and in spite of the fact that the tonnage of German shipping at present in existence is much less than is lost by the Allied and Associated Powers in consequence of the German aggression, the right thus recognized will be enforced on German ships and boats under the following conditions. The German government, on behalf of themselves and so as to bind all other persons interested, cede to the Allied and Associated Governments the property in all the German ships which are of 1,600 tons gross and upwards.

Paragraph 2. The German government will, within two months of the coming into force of the present treaty, deliver to the Reparations Committee all the ships mentioned in paragraph 1.

Disposal of Tonnage (The Reparations Commission)

The commission allowed all Allied and Associated governments to retain, as their own, all German vessels captured, detained or seized during the years of fighting up to 11 November 1918. Also no other government would be able to lay claim to these ships.

Thus, under the Armistice conditions and the Peace Treaty, Germany had been compelled to surrender ALL her merchant vessels of 1,600 tons or over. Her ships were divided among the Allied Powers.

HANSARD (The Parliamentary Secretary to the Minister of Shipping – Col. Leslie Wilson 11/12/19)

Up to the 7th December 1919, 355 vessels had been delivered for Allied management, of a total gross tonnage of 1,788,913. Of these, 230 vessels, of a total gross tonnage of 1,209,037 are under British management. The vessels under British management are allocated to shipping firms to manage on behalf of the Shipping Controller.

5

SURRENDERED VESSELS EITHER HANDED TO WHITE STAR LINE BY THE SHIPPING CONTROLLER FOR MANAGEMENT OR PURCHASED BY THE COMPANY FROM THE SHIPPING CONTROLLER

Hunslet

The *Hunslet* was built on the Tyne for D.D.G. 'Hansa' in Bremen and launched as the *Tannenfels*. Captured by a British destroyer in the Philippines in September 1914, she was returned to the UK in 1915 and renamed *Hunslet* by the Shipping Controller. White Star Line became her managers in January 1917. Sold to Woerman Line and renamed *Waganda* in 1921, she was scrapped in Germany in December 1932.

Ypiranga

Built for Hamburg–America Line, during the First World War she was laid up in Hamburg but in March 1919 she was ceded to Britain and, in April, came under White Star management. After repatriating troops that month she, in May, served the route to Australia until being laid up in Hull. After an overhaul she was bought by the Anchor Line in January 1921 and renamed *Assyria*. She was wrecked near Campbeltown and broken up in situ in 1950.

Hunslet: Built 1898. Gross tonnage 5,341. Captured as the *Tannenfels*.

Ypiranga: Built 1908. Gross tonnage 8,142. Managed by White Star for nearly two years.

Above and above left: Zeppelin: Built 1915. Gross tonnage 14,167. Only managed by White Star for one year.

Zeppelin

Launched on 9 June 1914 as *Zeppelin* for Nordeutscher Lloyd, she was laid up, structurally complete, at Vegesack, Germany, for the duration of the First World War until being surrendered to Britain in March 1919. She was managed by White Star until being sold to the Orient Line by the Ministry of Shipping in 1920 and renamed *Ormuz*. On 20 June 1934 she was wrecked and broken up in situ at Karmoy Island, Norway.

Below: Mobile: Built 1909. Gross tonnage 16,960. Not a satisfactory vessel.

Mobile

One of the first vessels to be surrendered under the Treaty of Versailles, built by Blohm & Voss, Hamburg, the twin-screw *Cleveland* stayed at Hamburg for the duration of the First World War. Offered in March 1919 by the Shipping Controller to the US Navy for trooping she was renamed *Mobile*. Chartered by White Star in 1920, she made only two return voyages for them, in White Star colours, from Liverpool to New York via Queenstown in August and September. White Star terminated her charter in October after these unsatisfactory voyages. She was broken up by Blohm & Voss Hamburg as the *Cleveland* (again) in April 1933.

Frankfurt

Ceded to Britain in March 1919, the twin-screw *Frankfurt* was built for Nordeutscher Lloyd. Put under White Star management, she was then sold to the Oriental Navigation Co. of Hong Kong and renamed *Sarvistan* in 1922. She was scrapped in Japan in 1931.

Frankfurt: Built 1899. Gross tonnage 7,431. Another vessel, initially managed, but later sold.

Alexandra Woermann

Originally built in 1898 as the *Bruxellesville* (1), she was transferred from one Belgian Line to another before being sold to the Woermann Line and renamed in 1901 for their Hamburg-West Africa service. During the First World War she acted as a transport in German coastal waters. However, she sank *UC91* in collision with the loss of sixteen lives in September 1918. Managed by White Star after being ceded to Britain, she made her only voyage under White Star management in May 1919 calling at Fremantle, en route to Melbourne, carrying over 400 dependents of Australian soldiers. Sold in 1920 to Ellerman's Wilson Line and renamed *Calypso* (3). Scrapped in Bruges in 1936. Single funnel, two masts. (Not illustrated)

Arabic (3)

Above: Arabic: Built 1908. Gross tonnage 16,786. Purchased from the Shipping Controller in 1920.

Below: Arabic in Red Star Line livery April 1927 to December 1929. (C.R. Hoffman)

The *Berlin* was launched at the A.G. Weser yard at Bremen for Nordeutscher Lloyd in November 1908. At the beginning of the First World War, she was converted into a minelayer for the German Navy and laid her first minefield between Northern Ireland and Scotland. The British battleship HMS *Audacious* was sunk by one of these mines on 26 October 1914. Many of the battleship's crew were rescued by White Star's *Olympic*. Unable to return to Germany due to a shortage of coal, the *Berlin* was interned in Norway for the next five years.

Under the Treaty of Versailles, the bulk of the German mercantile marine was turned over to the victorious allies. Berlin was purchased from the British Shipping Controller; White Star having decided that the purchase of ex-German vessels was more effective than new-ship construction. Ceded to Great Britain as a war reparation on 13 December 1919 and briefly managed by P&O, she was employed by White Star as *Arabic* (3) from 1921 to 1926 and transferred, within IMMC and without a name change, to Red Star. She was scrapped in Italy in 1931.

Homeric

Another vessel purchased by White Star from the British Shipping Controller, overseeing the distribution of seized German vessels, was the *Columbus*. She had been launched at the yards of F. Schichau for Nordeutscher Lloyd in December 1913. The yet to be completed vessel was renamed *Homeric* by White Star in June of 1920. She sailed from Danzig, having been laid up since the beginning of the First World War, to Hamburg on 19 December 1921. Her maximum speed of 18.5 knots made it difficult to fit her into the White Star's three-ship express service to New York. However, despite this lack of speed, the steadiness of *Homeric* in rough seas made her popular with the travelling public. In May of 1930, lessening passenger numbers contributed to her removal from the North Atlantic passenger service and she was placed on the popular short-cruise service from Liverpool and Southampton. Sold to Thos. W. Ward in February 1936 she was finally scrapped at Inverkeithing

Homeric: Built 1922. Gross tonnage 34,351. Arrival from Germany on 31 January 1922.

Homeric arriving at Inverkeithing for demolition on 27 February 1936.

Dutch illustration of the German liner *Columbus* at the Schichau yards in Danzig. Her final completion was put on hold as the First World War's military requirements took precedence.

Albertic

Ordered by Nordeutscher Lloyd as the *Munchen*, her keel was laid down in 1914 at Bremen in the A.G. Weser yard but all work on her was suspended until June 1919, after she had been ceded to the UK as war reparation under the Treaty of Versailles. She was launched in June 1920 and purchased from the Shipping Controller by the Royal Mail Group. Completed in March 1923, she was renamed *Ohio*. In February 1927 the *Ohio* was sold to White Star and renamed *Albertic*. After only eleven years, seven of them with White Star, the vessel arrived in Japan at the end of November 1934 for scrapping.

Left: *Munchen*: Built 1919. Gross tonnage 18,939. Became *Albertic* after Royal Mail's purchase of White Star from IMMCo.

Below: *Albertic* became a White Star liner for £1 million!

Bismarck: Built 1914. Gross tonnage 56,551. Launched by the grandaughter of Chancellor Bismarck, Countess Hanna von Bismarck. Kaiser Wilhelm II had to help her with the champagne bottle! (20 June 1914)

BISMARCK / MAJESTIC 2 / HMS CALEDONIA

Majestic (2)

Three giant liners had been planned by Hamburg–America Line to compete with White Star's Olympic-class liners. Each was slightly larger than her predecessor. The first was named *Imperator* and the third *Bismarck* (see opposite). At the end of the war both vessels were handed over to the UK as replacements for *Lusitania* and *Britannic*, respectively. Initially each company, Cunard and White Star, had a half-share of each ship but this was later changed to each company owning its ship outright.

Majestic, the world's largest ship, takes to the water for the first time.

The second of the vessels, *Vaterland*, spent the period until America's entry into the First World War in April 1917, trapped by the British Naval Blockade, in her US port of Hoboken, NJ. She was renamed USS *Leviathan* and retained by the US after the cessation of hostilities.

Bismarck, the third and last of the three vessels, was launched in June 1914 at Blohm & Voss's Hamburg yard and, until the advent of French Line's *Normandie* in 1935, would be the largest liner in the world. Owing to the demands made on the German ship-building industry, her completion was delayed throughout the First World War and she lay incomplete in Hamburg. The *Imperator* and the *Bismarck* were handed over to Britain and became Cunard's *Berengaria* and White Star's *Majestic*, respectively. The two shipping lines agreed, on 27 January 1921, to purchase jointly the two war reparation vessels from the British government for a total of one and a half million pounds.

The purchase from the Reparation committee was announced on 11 February 1921 but the joint purchase was not mentioned.

White Star, with the assistance of a technical team from Harland & Wolff, supervised the completion of *Bismarck*. Several incidents of suspected sabotage occurred during this time as, understandably, the Germans were reluctant to finish their vessel.

The shipyard workers at Blohm and Voss in Hamburg eventually completed the vessel. She was towed to the dry dock where her hull was cleaned and painted. Sir Bertram Hayes had been sent to Hamburg, to command her back to the UK, to discover that the name *Bismarck* had been painted. Once all the German hands had disembarked, the British crew started to paint her new name on the bow and stern.

On 30 December 1921 White Star Line had restored the title of 'Commodore'. They announced that Sir Bertram Hayes would be the next to hold that title when he assumed command of the *Majestic*.

Above left: Majestic incomplete at Hamburg. None of her funnels had been fitted at the end of the war. During her completion at Hamburg she was converted to oil-burning.

Below left: On the back of this illustration are the words 'Maiden Arrival Southampton'. I suspect that it shows *Majestic*'s departure from Hamburg as the tug is German and the funnel colours are still without their black tops. She departed Hamburg on 9 April 1922 and arrived Southampton on 10 April.

The *Bismarck* was renamed *Majestic* on 12 April 1922, after ten days of trials. She joined the White Star fleet and made her maiden voyage from Southampton to New York the following month.

White Star Line promotional card showing *Majestic*.

Above: *Majestic* in the floating dock at Southampton. Behind the Harbour Board Building to the left of the picture is Cunard's *Berengaria* which had once been *Imperator*, sister to *Bismarck/Majestic*.

Left: *Majestic* at New Docks Southampton Wednesday, 30 December 1936, before proceeding to Rosyth as Cadet Training Ship *Caledonia*.

The floating dock at Southampton was opened by the Prince of Wales on 27 June 1924. Before this, liners such as the *Majestic* would have had to go to Boston for dry-docking.

At the end of June 1932, the White Star and Cunard ten-year joint ownership of *Majestic* and *Berengaria* was mutually ended. It appears that *Berengaria* had earned more than *Majestic* during that period.

In 1936, after fourteen years of transatlantic service, she was laid up in Southampton before being sold for scrap in May. Bought from Thos. Ward by the Admiralty in July, she was converted into a Cadet Training Ship.

In order to facilitate her passage under the Forth Rail Bridge, her funnels (the last was a dummy) were shortened by the removal of the black tops, and she was renamed HMS *Caledonia*. In April 1937 she departed Southampton for Rosyth where she arrived two days later. At the commencement of the Second World War her cadets were sent ashore and she was moored out in the Firth of Forth. At the end of September 1939, she caught fire and sank on an even keel. By July 1943 the wreck had been partially broken up and it was raised and towed to the scrap yards at Inverkeithing.

Above: HMS *Caledonia* arrives in Scotland on 10 April 1937.

Below: HMS *Caledonia* (formerly *Majestic*) is helped by eight tugs to her berth at Rosyth, 10 April 1937.

THE FIRST WORLD WAR STANDARD BUILT SHIPS

During the First World War over 9 million tons of British ships were sunk. These sinkings peaked in the three months to June 1917 when over 1.4 million gross tons were lost.

At the end of 1916 a Shipping Controller was appointed by the British Government. He initiated a nationwide ship-building programme of vessels of a simple design with hulls and engines as standard.

All these vessels were given names pre-fixed by 'War'. At the end of fighting in 1918, many of these ships were sold to shipping companies and further designed to their new owner's requirements. The White Star Line purchased three of these vessels.

Gallic (2)

In 1918 twenty-two standard 'G' type vessels were built for the Shipping Controller. White Star Line purchased three. The first, *Gallic* (2), was coal-powered and launched as the *War Argus*. She was purchased in 1919, renamed and placed on the cargo service to Australia for the next fourteen years. Sold by White Star in 1933, she had several identities before being scrapped in Hong Kong in 1956.

Gallic 2: Built 1918. Gross tonnage 7,914. Leaving the Mersey for Brisbane, 1924. (B. & A. Feilden)

Bardic

Another of the 'G' type vessels, launched as the *War Priam* and renamed when purchased by White Star in 1919. She was sold in 1925.

Bardic: Built 1918. Gross tonnage 8,010. Went on to serve in the Second World War.

Delphic (2)

The third, and last, of the 'G' type vessels, purchased by IMMCo from the Shipping Controller. Launched in September 1918 as the *War Icarus*, she was initially purchased by Atlantic Transport Line and renamed *Mesaba* in 1919. Transferred to White Star in 1925, renamed *Delphic* and employed on the Australian service, she was sold in 1933 to Clan Line and renamed *Clan Farquar*. She was scrapped at Milford Haven in1933.

END GAME

At the end of October 1926, Lord Kylsant offered to acquire the Oceanic Steam Navigation Company (White Star Line), from IMMCo, to join his other shipping lines as part of his Royal Mail combine.

By the end of 1928 White Star had unsecured debts amounting to almost £10 million. The remainder of the Royal Mail combine was also in serious financial trouble.

The shares in Royal Mail began to slide in September 1929 and some directors began to publicly express their fears.

On 20 March 1930 Kylsant was given, by the Treasury, an ultimatum to restructure the company immediately. He still believed that any loans would be extended. He resigned as chairman of Harland & Wolff on 10 August amid concern over the financial condition of his Royal Mail Group.

In June 1932, the Australian service of White Star passed to Shaw Savill & Albion together with *Ionic*, *Ceramic* and *Zealandic*.

On the 24th of that month the now bankrupt empire of Lord Kylsant became a group of separate companies, including the White Star Line, each governed by its own directors.

The Royal Mail Group began to disintegrate by March 1933 and, at the end of that year the boards of O.S.N.Co. and Cunard approved the merger of their two companies forced upon them by the British Government. The merger was reported as being due to US immigration restrictions, Lord Kylsant's financial errors and the effects of the Depression.

The Cunard-White Star Line was registered on 11 May 1934.

The merger in effect brought about the end of the White Star Line. They contributed to the combined fleet the following vessels: *Majestic*, *Olympic*, *Homeric*, *Georgic*, *Britannic* (3), *Adriatic*, *Albertic*, *Laurentic* (2) *Doric* and *Calgaric*. By the start of the Second World War only *Britannic* (3) and *Georgic* remained in Cunard-White Star Lines hands. The remainder had either been sold, chartered or scrapped. Australian and New Zealand routes were given to Shaw Savill & Albion with *Ceramic* and *Ionic*.

Delphic: Built 1918. Gross tonnage 8,006. Only eight years with White Star! (Nautical Photo Agency)

6

WHITE STAR LINERS IN THE SECOND WORLD WAR

After the merger in 1934 of the White Star Line with the Cunard Steamship Company to form the Cunard–White Star Line, only two ships, *Britannic* and *Georgic*, were retained by the new company. The remainder were either quickly disposed of or went on to other companies.

Medic/Hektoria

In 1928 she was sold to N. Bugge in Tonsberg, converted into a whale factory ship and renamed *Hektoria*. Converted by the Ministry of War Transport to an oil tanker, she was torpedoed and sunk in convoy in the North Atlantic by *U608* with the loss of one life on 11 September 1942.

Runic (2)/New Sevilla

Sold in July 1930, she was converted into a whale factory ship and renamed *New Sevilla*. En route from the UK to Antarctica she was torpedoed and sunk by *U138* 30 miles off Galway in October 1940 with the loss of two lives although over 280 survived.

Above left: Medic/Hektoria.

Below left: Runic/New Sevilla.

Suevic/Skytteren

In October 1928 she was sold and converted into a whale factory ship and renamed *Skytteren*. In April 1940 she was interned in Gothenburg, Sweden. A chaotic attempt was made in April 1942 to break free of Swedish internment, with several other vessels, during which the *Skytteren* was scuttled by her own crew in order to avoid capture by waiting German vessels. She was just outside Swedish territorial waters and of the fifteen ships three were scuttled and six were sunk by enemy action.

Athenic/Pelagos

She was sold in 1928 and converted to a whale factory ship renamed *Pelagos*. Her conversion took three months during which she was also converted to oil-burning. She was captured by the German surface raider *Pinguin* on 15 January 1941, and after a varied career in the hands of the Kriegsmarine she was sunk in October 1944, raised in 1945 and scrapped in Hamburg in June 1962.

Athenic/Pelagos.

Suevic/Skytteren.

Ceramic.

Ceramic

After the merger of Cunard with White Star she was transferred in 1934 to Shaw Savill and Albion and continued on the Australian route. In 1936 she was modernised by Harland & Wolff in Govan with some glassed-in passenger accommodation and improvements to her crew quarters. Her original passenger capacity of 820 one class (cabin) had been reduced to 480 in 1936 and again, in 1938 to 340. February 1940 saw her requisitioned as a troopship but, owing to her speed, she did not sail in convoy. She maintained her route to Australia. During the night of 6/7 December 1942 she was torpedoed and sunk by *U155* off the Azores with the loss of 655 lives. There was one survivor, picked up by the submarine, Eric Munday a Royal Engineer sapper, who would spend the remainder of the war as a prisoner near Hamburg. (B. & A. Feilden)

Bardic/Marathon

After several owners and name changes, John Latsis of Piraeus purchased and renamed the vessel *Marathon* in 1937. She was sunk by the German battlecruiser *Scharnhorst* on 9 March 1941 en route to Alexandria from Swansea whilst a convoy straggler off the Cape Verde Islands. Her distress radio message and destruction allowed the bulk of the convoy to escape a similar fate.

Pittsburgh/Pennland (2)

Having been ordered for the American Line in 1913 at the yards of Harland & Wolff in Belfast, work was suspended in 1914 at the outbreak of the First World War as she was too far advanced to be converted into a troopship or cargo vessel. The vessel was finally launched in November 1920 for the White Star Line. Initially she was fitted with two sets of Topliss davits which were later removed in 1928 to be replaced by the usual Welin davits. She was originally to have been coal-fired but prior to being handed over was converted to oil-burning. The rear funnel was a dummy.

In January 1925 she operated Red Star Line's Antwerp–New York service via Southampton and Cherbourg and, in 1926, was renamed *Pennland* (2). Prior to this she always carried an American Line name, *Pittsburgh*, despite being painted in White Star Line colours.

After the collapse of the Red Star Line in November 1934 she was sold, in January 1935 to Arnold Bernstein for his Red Star Line GmbH. In 1937 Bernstein, being Jewish, was arrested by the Nazi authorities and imprisoned. His two ships, *Pennland* and *Westernland*, were sold to Holland America Line but continued to operate the service from Antwerp to New York via Le Havre, Southampton and Halifax. At the commencement of the Second World War, she carried the neutrality notification of 'Rotterdam' along each side but after the German invasion of Belgium in 1940 the *Pennland*, having sailed from Antwerp, returned to Liverpool and was chartered to the UK's Ministry of War Transport as a troopship. As such she was bombed seven times and sunk by German aircraft with the loss of three lives, in the Mediterranean, in April 1941.

Top right: Bardic/Marathon.

Centre right: Pittsburgh/Pennland: Built 1922. Gross tonnage 16, 322.

Bottom right: Pittsburgh/Pennland in Red Star Line colours. (Kirk card)

Pennland. Arnold Bernstein's Red Star Line 1935–39.

Zealandic

Whilst on the way to Chatham to be reconverted from a dummy aircraft carrier back to a refrigerated cargo vessel, on 2 June 1941, trying to avoid German aircraft she hit the wreck of the tanker *Ahamo* near Cromer. The next night she sank after being torpedoed by German E-boats. (Not illustrated)

Regina/Westernland

In August 1920 she returned to Harland & Wolff in Glasgow to be restored to her original drawings with Topliss davits, similar to her sisters *Doric* and *Pittsburgh*, and two funnels. Originally employed on White Star's joint service to Canada with the Dominion Line she was switched, by IMMC, to the Red Star Line service and renamed *Westernland* early in 1930. Sold, with *Pennland*, to Holland America Line in 1939, she had also been owned by Arnold Bernstein. Having escaped to Britain after the German invasion of Holland she briefly became the HQ vessel of the Dutch government-in-exile. Bought by the British Admiralty in 1942, she was converted into a depot ship for destroyers in 1943, still a coal-burner! After the Second World War was over, Cunard–White Star thought that the *Westernland* could be converted to a passenger vessel on the Canadian run but her age was against her. She was laid up and in 1947 was scrapped at Blyth.

Regina: Built 1920. Gross tonnage 16,313. In Dominion Line colours, on her maiden voyage, 16 March 1922, having been restored to her original design.

Arnold Bernstein's *Westernland* Red Star Line GmbH.

Regina after being transferred to White Star Line on 12 December 1925. A Leyland vessel, with a Dominion name, painted in White Star livery and operated by Red Star!

Laurentic (2)

She would be the only vessel built for the White Star Line by Harland & Wolff, Belfast on a 'fixed price' basis rather than the usual 'cost plus' basis. This was because of the economics created by the Depression and the financial woes of the ailing White Star Line. The *Laurentic* was launched in June 1927 and made her first voyage for White Star, in April 1928, to Canada. Still coal-powered and now owned by the newly merged Cunard–White Star Line, she was in collision with Blue Star Line's *Napier Star* in the Irish Sea in August 1935. Laid up, she may have been destined for the scrapyard after her collision, except for one trooping journey to Palestine, until September 1939 when she was requisitioned by the Admiralty, towed to Devonport dockyard, converted to an Armed Merchant Cruiser and armed with 5.5-inch and 4-inch guns. During this conversion her mainmast and the majority of her lifeboats were removed and her hull and funnels painted black. In November 1940 she went to the assistance of the Elder & Fyffes vessel *Casanare*, which had been torpedoed by *U99* off the Bloody Foreland. She herself was also torpedoed and Blue Funnel's *Patroclus*, also an Armed Merchant Cruiser, went to her aid. The *Patroclus* was torpedoed and sunk. The total tonnage of the three lost ships came to over 35,000! Kretschmer, the commander of the U-boat, became only the second U-boat commander to sink over 200,000 tons.

Laurentic: Built 1927. Gross tonnage 18,724. Completed at the beginning of White Star's financial problems and coal-powered!

Right: *Laurentic* (2) in Gladstone graving dock Liverpool, after collision with the Napier Star in August 1935.

Below: Blue Star Line's *Napier Star* (10,855 tons). Torpedoed and sunk 18 December 1940. (B. & A. Feilden)

Above: Britannic: Built 1930. Gross tonnage 26,943. Fitting out at Harland & Wolff, Belfast. (Nautical Photo Agency)

Left: Britannic dressed overall, on her maiden voyage 28 June 1930. (B. & A. Feilden)

Britannic (3)

Launched in August 1929 she, with her sister *Georgic* (2), would be the last vessel built for the White Star Line. The forward funnel was a dummy which contained the radio cabin and the engineers' smoke room. Discernible from her sister in that she had a square-fronted bridge, both vessels were motorships with two squat funnels.

Britannic sailed on her maiden voyage in June 1930 on the Liverpool–New York service. Absorbed into the Cunard-White Star Line fleet in May 1934 she operated from London to New York. In August 1939 she was converted into a troopship for 3,000, later increased to 5,000. Her sister *Georgic* remained on civilian service but was moved from London to Liverpool. By January 1940 she had been painted grey. Between 1939 and 1945 *Britannic* transported nearly 180,000 troops and had travelled 376,000 miles. In 1946 she continued her trooping, but mostly repatriation to the Far East. Returning to Cunard–White Star after her war service, she was finally scrapped at Inverkeithing in 1961. She was White Star Line's last vessel and throughout her career she had been owned by White Star, Cunard–White Star and Cunard Line.

Britannic joined the Cunard-White Star fleet after the merger in 1934.

Georgic (2)

The last liner to be built for the White Star Line, the *Georgic* was launched in November 1931 and made her maiden voyage in June 1932. By March 1940 she had made five return voyages to New York from Liverpool since September 1939, before being requisitioned as a troopship in March 1940. Despite carrying troops, her convoy to Port Tewfik had to be almost abandoned in May 1941 when the battleship *Rodney* was called to participate in the hunt for, and destruction of, the German battleship *Bismarck*.

Whilst at Port Tewfik the *Georgic* was very badly damaged by German bombs, caught fire and sank in shallow water. There then followed an incredibly successful salvage operation. The hulk was raised in the following October (1941) and towed to Port Sudan after having her hull plugged. Towed first to Karachi and then Bombay she finally departed for Liverpool on 20 January 1943 and then on to Belfast. In December 1944, now owned by the Ministry of War Transport, she came away from Belfast with only one funnel and just one shortened foremast. She trooped and repatriated for the remainder of the war and, in 1949, was involved in the 'assisted passage' scheme to Sydney. Chartered to Cunard for transatlantic service from 1950 until 1954, she made two more trooping voyages before being scrapped at Faslane in February 1956.

Georgic: Built 1930. Gross tonnage 27,759. Shortly after, if not on, her maiden voyage as dressed overall. (B. & A. Feilden)

Left: Georgic, now owned by the Ministry of War Transport and managed by Cunard-White Star.

Below: Finally, after the end of the Second World War, *Georgic* was chartered to the Cunard Line but still in White Star colours.

BIBLIOGRAPHY

Hawes, Duncan. *Merchant Fleets in Profile 2: The Ships of the Cunard, American, Red Star, Inman, Leyland, Dominion, Atlantic Transport and White Star Lines* (Patrick Stephens Ltd, 1979)

Hayes, Sir Bertram K.C.M.G., D.S.O. *Hull Down: Reminiscences of Wind-jammers, Troops and Travellers* (The Macmillan Company, 1925)

de Kerbrech, Richard. *Ships of the White Star Line* (Ian Allen Publishing Ltd, 2009)

Streater, Les. *White Star Line: The Company & The Ships* (Maritime Publishing, 2012)

ACKNOWLEDGEMENTS

I am most grateful to all those who have supported my enthusiasm for the subject and have also benefited me with their knowledge and technical support.

Sir Neville Purvis K.C.B. Vice Admiral for kindly agreeing to write the foreword.

Mrs Janina Stamps for her untiring patience and technological skills.

Ms Patti Aronsson and Mr Emanuel Silberstein for allowing me the use, many times, of their beautiful home and encouragement in all things White Star!

Ms Caroline Mylon and Mr Iain Yardley for, once again, their continued support of my endeavours.

Ms Amy Rigg (Commissioning Editor) and all at The History Press for their confidence in me, superb design abilities and knowledge.

Mr Neil Egginton for his amazing depictions of White Star vessels in the First World War.

MORE FROM
THE HISTORY PRESS

THE
UNSEEN
OLYMPIC
THE SHIP IN RARE ILLUSTRATIONS

PATRICK MYLON

978 0 7509 8267 2

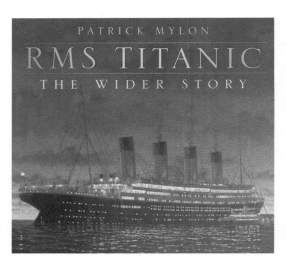

PATRICK MYLON
RMS TITANIC
THE WIDER STORY

978 0 7509 6136 3

THE WHITE STAR COLLECTION

A SHIPPING LINE IN POSTCARDS
PATRICK MYLON

978 0 7524 5937 0